THE BOOKS OF
AMERICAN
NEGRO SPIRITUALS

Books by James Weldon Johnson:

SAINT PETER RELATES AN INCIDENT
(Selected Poems)

NEGRO AMERICANS, WHAT NOW?

GOD'S TROMBONES
(Seven Negro Sermons in Verse)

ALONG THIS WAY
(Autobiography)

BLACK MANHATTAN

THE AUTOBIOGRAPHY OF AN EX-COLORED MAN
(Fiction)

———

Edited and Arranged by J. Rosamond Johnson:

ROLLING ALONG IN SONG
A Chronological Survey of American Negro Music
(with arrangements of 87 songs)

The Books of American Negro Spirituals

INCLUDING

The Book of American Negro Spirituals

AND

The Second Book of Negro Spirituals

JAMES WELDON JOHNSON

and

J. ROSAMOND JOHNSON

DA CAPO PRESS

A Member of the Perseus Books Group

This Da Capo Press paperback edition of *The Books of American Negro Spirituals* is an unabridged republication of the editions published in New York in 1925 and 1926 as two separate volumes, and republished in 1969 as a single volume. It is reprinted by arrangement with The Viking Press.

Cataloging in Publication data is available from the Library of Congress.

ISBN 0-306-81202-9

Published by Da Capo Press
A Member of the Perseus Books Group
http://www.dacapopress.com

Alphabetical List of Spirituals

(In the following pages, the two Books of American Negro Spirituals have been reproduced exactly in their original form. Hence the page numbering begins again in the middle of this volume. The roman numeral in front of each page number in the list below indicates whether the reference is to the first or second half of this volume.)

ALPHABETICAL LIST OF SPIRITUALS

THE BOOK OF AMERICAN
NEGRO SPIRITUALS

THE BOOK OF AMERICAN NEGRO SPIRITUALS

Edited with an introduction by
JAMES WELDON JOHNSON

Musical arrangements by
J. ROSAMOND JOHNSON

Additional numbers by
LAWRENCE BROWN

*To those through whose efforts these
songs have been collected, preserved
and given to the world this book
is lovingly dedicated.*

CONTENTS

CONTENTS

THE BOOK OF AMERICAN
NEGRO SPIRITUALS

PREFACE

O BLACK AND UNKNOWN BARDS

O black and unknown bards of long ago,
How came your lips to touch the sacred fire?
How, in your darkness, did you come to know
The power and beauty of the minstrel's lyre?
Who first from midst his bonds lifted his eyes?
Who first from out the still watch, lone and long,
Feeling the ancient faith of prophets rise
Within his dark-kept soul, burst into song?

Heart of what slave poured out such melody
As "Steal away to Jesus"?   On its strains
His spirit must have nightly floated free,
Though still about his hands he felt his chains.
Who heard great "Jordan roll"?   Whose starward eye
Saw chariot "swing low"?   And who was he
That breathed that comforting, melodic sigh,
"Nobody knows de trouble I see"?

What merely living clod, what captive thing,
Could up toward God through all its darkness grope,
And find within its deadened heart to sing
These songs of sorrow, love and faith, and hope?
How did it catch that subtle undertone,
That note in music heard not with the ears?
How sound the elusive reed so seldom blown,
Which stirs the soul or melts the heart to tears?

Not that great German master in his dream
Of harmonies that thundered amongst the stars
At the creation, ever heard a theme
Nobler than "Go down, Moses."   Mark its bars,
How like a mighty trumpet call they stir

11

PREFACE

The blood. Such are the notes that men have sung
Going to valorous deeds; such tones there were
That helped make history when time was young.

There is a wide, wide wonder in it all,
That from degraded rest and servile toil
The fiery spirit of the seer should call
These simple children of the sun and soil.
O black slave singers, gone forgot, unfamed,
You—you alone, of all the long, long line
Of those who've sung untaught, unknown, unnamed,
Have stretched out upward, seeking the divine.

You sang not deeds of heroes or of kings;
No chant of bloody war, no exulting pæan
Of arms-won triumphs; but your humble strings
You touched in chord with music empyrean.
You sang far better than you knew; the songs
That for your listeners' hungry hearts sufficed
Still live,—but more than this to you belongs:
You sang a race from wood and stone to Christ.

It was in the above lines, which appeared in the *Century Magazine* nearly twenty years ago, that I tried to voice my estimate and appreciation of the Negro Spirituals and to celebrate the unknown black bards who created them. As the years go by and I understand more about this music and its origin the miracle of its production strikes me with increasing wonder. It would have been a notable achievement if the white people who settled this country, having a common language and heritage, seeking liberty in a new land, faced with the task of conquering untamed nature, and stirred with the hope of building an empire, had created a body of folk music comparable to the Negro Spirituals. But from whom did these songs spring—these songs unsurpassed among the folk songs of the world and, in the poignancy of their beauty, unequalled?

In 1619 a Dutch vessel landed twenty African natives at Jamestown, Virginia. They were quickly bought up by the colonial settlers. This was the beginning of the African slave trade in the American Colonies. To supply this trade Africa was raped of millions of men, women and

PREFACE

children. [1] As many as survived the passage were immediately thrown into slavery. These people came from various localities in Africa. They did not all speak the same language. Here they were, suddenly cut off from the moorings of their native culture, scattered without regard to their old tribal relations, having to adjust themselves to a completely alien civilization, having to learn a strange language, and, moreover, held under an increasingly harsh system of slavery; yet it was from these people this mass of noble music sprang; this music which is America's only folk music and, up to this time, the finest distinctive artistic contribution she has to offer the world. It is strange!

I have termed this music noble, and I do so without any qualifications. Take, for example, *Go Down, Moses;* there is not a nobler theme in the whole musical literature of the world. If the Negro had voiced himself in only that one song, it would have been evidence of his nobility of soul. Add to this *Deep River, Stand Still Jordan, Walk Together Children, Roll Jordan Roll, Ride On King Jesus,* and you catch a spirit that is a little more than mere nobility; it is something akin to majestic grandeur. The music of these songs is always noble and their sentiment is always exalted. Never does their philosophy fall below the highest and purest motives of the heart. And this might seem stranger still.

Perhaps there will be no better point than this at which to say that all the true Spirituals possess dignity. It is, of course, pardonable to smile at the naïveté often exhibited in the words, but it should be remembered that in scarcely no instance was anything humorous intended. When it came to the use of words, the maker of the song was struggling as best he could under his limitations in language and, perhaps, also under a misconstruction or misapprehension of the facts in his source of material, generally the Bible. And often, like his more literary poetic brothers, he had to do a good many things to get his rhyme in. But almost always he was in dead earnest. There are doubtless many persons who have heard these songs sung only on the vaudeville or theatrical stage and have laughed uproariously at them because they were presented in humorous vein. Such people

[1] For a history of the slave trade and its horrors see "The Suppression of the Slave Trade" by W. E. B. Du Bois.

have no conception of the Spirituals. They probably thought of them as a new sort of ragtime or minstrel song. These Spirituals cannot be properly appreciated or understood unless they are clothed in their primitive dignity.

No space will here be given to a rehearsal of the familiar or easily accessible facts regarding the origin and development of folk music in general. Nor will any attempt be made at a discussion of the purely technical questions of music involved. A thorough exposition of this latter phase of the subject will be found in H. E. Krehbiel's *Afro-American Folksongs*. There Mr. Krehbiel makes an analysis of the modes, scales and intervals of these songs and a comparative study between them and the same features of other folksongs. Here it is planned, rather, to relate regarding these songs as many facts as possible that will be of interest to the general lover of music and serve to present adequately this collection. Instead of dissecting this music we hope to recreate around it as completely as we can its true atmosphere and place it in a proper setting for those who already love the Spirituals and those who may come to know them.

Although the Spirituals have been overwhelmingly accredited to the Negro as his own, original creation, nevertheless, there have been one or two critics who have denied that they were original either with the Negro or in themselves, and a considerable number of people have eagerly accepted this view. The opinion of these critics is not sound. It is not based upon scientific or historical inquiry. Indeed, it can be traced ultimately to a prejudiced attitude of mind, to an unwillingness to concede the creation of so much pure beauty to a people they wish to feel is absolutely inferior. Once that power is conceded, the idea of absolute inferiority cannot hold. These critics point to certain similarities in structure between the Spirituals and the folk music of other peoples, ignoring the fact that there are such similarities between all folksongs. The Negro Spirituals are as distinct from the folksongs of other peoples as those songs are from each other; and, perhaps, more so. One needs to be only ordinarily familiar with the folk music of the world to see that this is so.

14

PREFACE

The statement that the Spirituals are imitations made by the Negro of other music that he heard is an absurdity. What music did American Negroes hear to imitate? They certainly had no opportunity to go to Scotland or Russia or Scandinavia and bring back echoes of songs from those lands. Some of them may have heard a few Scotch songs in this country, but it is inconceivable that this great mass of five or six hundred Negro songs could have sprung from such a source. What music then was left for them to imitate? Some have gone so far as to say that they caught snatches of airs from the French Opera at New Orleans; but the songs of the Negroes who fell most directly under that influence are of a type distinct from the Spirituals. It was in localities far removed from New Orleans that the great body of Spirituals were created and sung. There remains then the music which the American Negroes heard their masters sing; chiefly religious music. Now if ignorant Negroes evolved such music as *Deep River, Steal Away to Jesus, Somebody's Knockin' at Yo' Do', I Couldn't Hear Nobody Pray* and *Father Abraham* by listening to their masters sing gospel hymns, it does not detract from the achievement but magnifies it.

Regarding the origin of this music, I myself have referred to the "miracle" of its production. And it is easier to believe the miracle than some of the explanations of it that are offered. Most difficult of all is it to believe that the Negro slaves were indebted to their white masters for the sources of these songs. The white people among whom the slaves lived did not originate anything comparable even to the mere titles of the Spirituals. In truth, the power to frame the poetic phrases that make the titles of so many of the Spirituals betokens the power to create the songs. Consider the sheer magic of:

> Swing Low Sweet Chariot
> I've Got to Walk My Lonesome Valley
> Steal Away to Jesus
> Singing With a Sword in My Hand
> Rule Death in His Arms
> Ride on King Jesus
> We Shall Walk Through the Valley in Peace
> The Blood Came Twinklin' Down

15

PREFACE

Deep River
Death's Goin' to Lay His Cold, Icy Hand on Me

and confess that none but an artistically endowed people could have evoked it.

No one has even expressed a doubt that the poetry of the titles and text of the Spirituals is Negro in character and origin, no one else has dared to lay claim to it; why then doubt the music? There is a slight analogy here to the Shakespeare-Bacon controversy. The Baconians in their amazement before the transcendent greatness of the plays declare that Shakespeare could not possibly have written them; he was not scholar enough; he did not know enough Greek; no mere play actor could be gentleman enough to be so familiar with the ways of the court and royalty; no mere play actor could be philosopher enough to know all the hidden springs of human motives and conduct. Then they pick a man who fills these requirements and accounts for the phenomenon of the crowning glory of the English tongue. Lord Francis Bacon, they say, wrote the plays but did not claim them because it was not creditable for a gentleman to be a playwright. However, though it was creditable for a gentleman of the age to be a poet, they do not explain why Lord Bacon did not claim the poems. And it is easy to see that the hand that wrote the poems could write the plays.

Nobody thought of questioning the Negro's title as creator of this music until its beauty and value were demonstrated. The same thing, in a greater degree, has transpired with regard to the Negro as the originator of America's popular medium of musical expression; in fact, to such a degree that it is now completely divorced from all ideas associated with the Negro. Still, for several very good reasons, it will not be easy to do that with the Spirituals.

When the Fisk Jubilee Singers [2] toured Europe they sang in England, Scotland and Germany, spending eight months in the latter country. Their concerts were attended by the most cultured and so-

[2] The Jubilee Singers of Fisk University first introduced the Spirituals to the public. From 1871 to 1875 they gave many concerts in the United States, and made two tours of Europe. They raised a net sum of more than $150,000 for the University. Jubilee Hall is one of the monuments of their efforts.

16

phisticated people as well as the general public. In England they sang before Queen Victoria, and in Germany the Emperor was among those who listened to them. Music critics paid special attention to the singers and their songs. The appearance of the Jubilee Singers in Europe constituted both an artistic sensation and a financial success, neither of which results could have been attained had their songs been mere imitations of European folk music or adaptations of European airs.

The Spirituals are purely and solely the creation of the American Negro; that is, as much so as any music can be the pure and sole creation of any particular group. And their production, although seemingly miraculous, can be accounted for naturally. The Negro brought with him from Africa his native musical instinct and talent, and that was no small endowment to begin with.

Many things are now being learned about Africa. It is being learned and recognized that the great majority of Africans are in no sense "savages"; that they possess a civilization and a culture, primitive it is true but in many respects quite adequate; that they possess a folk literature that is varied and rich; that they possess an art that is quick and sound. Among those who know about art it is generally recognized that the modern school of painting and sculpture in Europe and America is almost entirely the result of the direct influence of African art, following the discovery that it was art.[3] Not much is yet known about African music, and, perhaps, for the reason that the conception of music by the Africans is not of the same sort as the conception of music by the people of Western Europe and the United

[3] "Of all the arts of the primitive races, the art of the African Negro savage is the one which has had a positive influence upon the art of our epoch. From its principles of plastic representation a new art movement has evolved. The point of departure and the resting point of our abstract representation are based on the art of that race. It is certain that before the introduction of the plastic principles of Negro art, abstract representations did not exist among Europeans. Negro art has reawakened in us the feeling for abstract form; it has brought into our art the means to express our purely sensorial feelings in regard to form, or to find new form in our ideas. The abstract representation of modern art is unquestionably the offspring of the Negro Art, which has made us conscious of the subjective state, obliterated by objective education." *African Negro Art—Its Influence on Modern Art*, M. de Zayas.

17

PREFACE

States. Generally speaking, the European concept of music is melody and the African concept is rhythm. Melody has, relatively, small place in African music, and harmony still less; but in rhythms African music is beyond comparison with any other music in the world. Krehbiel, after visiting the Dahomey Village at the World's Fair in Chicago, and witnessing the natives dance to the accompaniment of choral singing and the beating of their drums, wrote of them:

"The players showed the most remarkable rhythmical sense and skill that ever came under my notice. Berlioz, in his supremest effort with his army of drummers, produced nothing to compare in artistic interest with the harmonious drumming of these savages. The fundamental effect was a combination of double and triple time, the former kept by the singers, the latter by the drummers, but it is impossible to convey the idea of the wealth of detail achieved by the drummers by means of exchange of the rhythms, syncopation of both simultaneously, and dynamic devices. Only by making a score of the music could this be done. I attempted to make such a score by enlisting the help of the late John C. Fillmore, experienced in Indian music, but we were thwarted by the players who, evidently divining our purpose when we took out our notebooks, mischievously changed their manner of playing as soon as we touched pencil to paper. I was forced to the conclusion that in their command of the element, which in the musical art of the ancient Greeks stood higher than either melody or harmony, the best composers of today were the veriest tyros compared with these black savages."[4]

The musical genius of the African has not become so generally recognized as his genius in sculpture and design, and yet it has had a wide influence on the music of the world. Friedenthal points out that African Negroes have a share in the creation of one of the best known and most extended musical forms, the Habanera.[5] This form which is popularly known as the chief characteristic of Spanish music is a combination of Spanish melody and African rhythm. Friedenthal, regarding this combination, says:

Here stand these two races facing each other, both highly musical but reared in different worlds of music. Little wonder that the Spaniards quickly took

[4] H. E. Krehbiel, *Afro-American Folksongs*. New York, 1914.
[5] Alfred Friedenthal, *Stimmen der Völker*. Berlin, 1911.

18

advantage of these remarkable rhythms and incorporated them into their own music. . . . The melody of the Habanera came out of Middle or Southern Spain, and the rhythm which accompanies it had its origin in Africa. We therefore have, in a way, the union of Spanish spirit and African technique." [6]

The rhythm of the Habanera reduced to its simplest is:

and is the rhythm characteristic of Spanish and Latin-American music. A considerable portion of Bizet's opera, Carmen, is based on this originally African rhythm.

Further, regarding the musical genius of the Africans, Friedenthal says: "Now the African Negroes possess great musical talent. It must be admitted, though, that in the invention of melodies, they do not come up to the European standard, but the greater is their capacity as inventors of rhythms. The talent exhibited by the Bantus in contriving the most complex rhythms is nothing short of marvelous." [7]

Now, the Negro in America had his native musical endowment to begin with; and the Spirituals possess the fundamental characteristics of African music. They have a striking rhythmic quality, and show a marked similarity to African songs in form and intervallic structure. But the Spirituals, upon the base of the primitive rhythms, go a step in advance of African music through a higher melodic and an added harmonic development. For the Spirituals are not merely melodies. The melodies of many of them, so sweet or strong or even weird, are wonderful, but hardly more wonderful than the harmonies. One has never experienced the full effect of these songs until he has heard their harmonies in the part singing of a large number of Negro voices. I shall say more about this question of harmony later. But what led to this advance by the American Negro beyond his primitive music? Why did he not revive and continue the beating out of complex rhythms on tom toms and drums while he uttered barbaric and martial cries to

[6] Alfred Friedenthal, *Musik, Tanz und Dichtung bei den Kreolen Amerikas.*
[7] Alfred Friedenthal, *Stimmen der Völker.* Berlin, 1911.

their accompaniment? It was because at the precise and psychic moment there was blown through or fused into the vestiges of his African music the spirit of Christianity as he knew Christianity.

At the psychic moment there was at hand the precise religion for the condition in which he found himself thrust. Far from his native land and customs, despised by those among whom he lived, experiencing the pang of the separation of loved ones on the auction block, knowing the hard task master, feeling the lash, the Negro seized Christianity, the religion of compensations in the life to come for the ills suffered in the present existence, the religion which implied the hope that in the next world there would be a reversal of conditions, of rich man and poor man, of proud and meek, of master and slave. The result was a body of songs voicing all the cardinal virtues of Christianity—patience—forbearance—love—faith—and hope—through a necessarily modified form of primitive African music. The Negro took complete refuge in Christianity, and the Spirituals were literally forged of sorrow in the heat of religious fervor. They exhibited, moreover, a reversion to the simple principles of primitive, communal Christianity.

The thought that the Negro might have refused or failed to adopt Christianity—and there were several good reasons for such an outcome, one being the vast gulf between the Christianity that was preached to him and the Christianity practiced by those who preached it—leads to some curious speculations. One thing is certain, there would have been no Negro Spirituals. His musical instinct would doubtless have manifested itself; but is it conceivable that he could have created a body of songs in any other form so unique in the musical literature of the world and with such a powerful and universal appeal as the Spirituals? Indeed, the question arises, would he have been able to survive slavery in the way in which he did? It is not possible to estimate the sustaining influence that the story of the trials and tribulations of the Jews as related in the Old Testament exerted upon the Negro. This story at once caught and fired the imaginations of the Negro bards, and they sang, sang their hungry listeners into a firm faith that as God saved Daniel in the lion's den, so would He save them; as God preserved the Hebrew children in the fiery furnace, so would He preserve them; as God delivered Israel out of bondage in Egypt, so would He deliver them. How much this firm faith had to do with the Negro's physical and spiritual survival of two and a half centuries of slavery cannot be known.

Thus it was by sheer spiritual forces that African chants were metamorphosed into the Spirituals; that upon the fundamental throb of African rhythms were reared those reaches of melody that rise above earth and soar into the pure, ethereal blue. And this is the miracle of the creation of the Spirituals.

As is true of all folksongs, there are two theories as to the manner in which the Spirituals were "composed"; whether they were the spontaneous outburst and expression of the group or chiefly the work of individual talented makers. I doubt that either theory is exclusively correct. The Spirituals are true folksongs and originally intended only for group singing. Some of them may be the spontaneous creation of the group, but my opinion is that the far greater part of them is the work of talented individuals influenced by the pressure and reaction of the group. The responses, however, may be more largely the work of the group in action; it is likely that they simply burst forth. It is also true that many of these songs have been modified and varied as they have been sung by different groups in different localities. This process is still going on. Sometimes we find two or more distinct variations of the melody of a song. There are also the interchange and substitution of lines. Yet, it is remarkable that these variations and changes are as few as they are, considering the fact that these songs have been for generations handed down from ear to ear and by word of mouth. Variations in melody are less common than interchange of lines. The committing to memory of all the leading lines constituted quite a feat, for they run high into the hundreds; so sometimes the leader's memory failed him and he would have to improvise or substitute. This substituting accounts for a good deal of the duplication of leading lines.

In the old days there was a definitely recognized order of bards, and to some degree it still persists. These bards gained their recognition by achievement. They were makers of songs and leaders of singing. They had to possess certain qualifications: a gift of melody, a talent for poetry, a strong voice, and a good memory. Here we have a demand for a great many gifts in one individual; yet, they were all necessary. The recognized bard required the ability to make up the appealing tune, to fashion the graphic phrase, to pitch the tune true and lead it clearly, and to remember all the lines. There was, at least, one leader of singing in every congregation but makers of songs were less common. My memory of childhood goes back to a great leader of singing, "Ma" White, and a maker of songs, "Singing" Johnson. "Ma" White was an excellent laundress and a busy woman, but each church meeting found her in her place ready to lead the singing, whenever the formal choir and organ did not usurp her ancient rights. I can still recall her shrill, plaintive voice quavering above the others. Memory distinctly brings back her singing of *We Are Climbing Jacob's Ladder, Keep Me From Sinking Down,* and *We Shall Walk Through the Valley in Peace.* Even as a child my joy in hearing her sing these songs was deep and full. She was the recognized leader of spiritual singing in the congregation to which she belonged and she took her duties seriously. One of her duties was to "sing-down" a long-winded or uninteresting speaker at love feasts or experience meetings, and even to cut short a prayer of undue length by raising a song. (And what a gentle method of gaining relief from a tiresome speaker. Why shouldn't it be generally adopted today?) "Ma" White had a great reputation as a leader of singing, a reputation of which she was proud and jealous. She knew scores of Spirituals, but I do not think she ever "composed" any songs.

On the other hand, singing was "Singing" Johnson's only business. He was not a fixture in any one congregation or community, but went from one church to another, singing his way. I can recall that his periodical visits caused a flutter of excitement akin to that caused by the visit of a famed preacher. These visits always meant the hearing and learning of something new. I recollect how the congregation would hang on his voice for a new song—new, at least to them. They listened through, some of them joining in waveringly. The quicker ears soon caught the melody and words. The whole congregation easily learned the response, which is generally unvarying. They sang at first hesitantly, but seizing the song quickly, made up for hesitation by added gusto in the response. Always the strong voice of the leader corrected errors until the song was perfectly learned. "Singing" Johnson must have derived his support in somewhat the same way as the preachers,—part of a collection, food and lodging. He doubtless spent his leisure time in originating new words and melodies and new lines for old songs. "Singing" Johnson is one of the indelible pictures on my mind. A small but stocky, dark-brown man was he, with one eye, and possessing a clear, strong, high-pitched voice. Not as striking a figure as some of the great Negro preachers I used to see and hear, but at camp meetings, revivals, and on special occasions only slightly less important than any of them. A maker of songs and a wonderful leader of singing. A man who could improvise lines on the moment. A great judge of the appropriate song to sing; and with a delicate sense of when to come to the preacher's support after a climax in the sermon had been reached by breaking in with a line or two of a song that expressed a certain sentiment, often just a single line. "Singing" Johnson always sang with his eyes, or eye, closed, and indicated the tempo by swinging his head and body. When he warmed to his work it was easy to see that he was transported and utterly oblivious to his surroundings.

"Singing" Johnson was of the line of the mightier bards of an earlier day, and he exemplified how they worked and how the Spirituals were "composed." These bards, I believe, made the original inventions of story and song, which in turn were influenced or modified by the group in action.

In form the Spirituals often run strictly parallel with African songs, incremental leading lines and choral iteration. Krehbiel quotes from Denham and Clapperton's *Narrative of Travels in Northern and Central Africa*, the following song by Negro bards of Bornou in praise of their Sultan:

> Give flesh to the hyenas at daybreak—
>   Oh, the broad spears!
> The spear of the Sultan is the broadest—
>   Oh, the broad spears!

PREFACE

I behold thee now, I desire to see none other—
  Oh, the broad spears!
My horse is as tall as a high wall—
  Oh, the broad spears!
He will fight ten—he fears nothing!
  Oh, the broad spears!
He has slain ten, the guns are yet behind—
  Oh, the broad spears!
The elephant of the forest brings me what I want—
  Oh, the broad spears!
Like unto thee, so is the Sultan—
  Oh, the broad spears!
Be brave! Be brave, my friends and kinsmen—
  Oh, the broad spears!
God is great! I wax fierce as a beast of prey—
  Oh, the broad spears!
God is great! Today those I wished for are come—
  Oh, the broad spears!

Or take this beautiful song found in one of the Bantu folk-tales. It is the song of an old woman standing at the edge of the river with a babe in her arms, singing to coax back the child's mother, who has been enchanted and taken by the river. The tale is *The Story of Tangalimlibo,* and the song runs as follows:

It is crying, it is crying,
  Sihamba Ngenyanga.
The child of the walker by moonlight,
  Sihamba Ngenyanga.
It was done intentionally by people, whose names cannot be mentioned
  Sihamba Ngenyanga.
They sent her for water during the day,
  Sihamba Ngenyanga.
She tried to dip it with the milk basket, and then it sank,
  Sihamba Ngenyanga.
Tried to dip it with the ladle, and then it sank,
  Sihamba Ngenyanga.
Tried to dip it with the mantle, and then it sank,
  Sihamba Ngenyanga.

24

PREFACE

Compare these African songs with the American Spiritual, *Oh, Wasn't Dat a Wide Ribber*:

> Oh, de Ribber of Jordan is deep and wide,
>   One mo' ribber to cross.
> I don't know how to get on de other side,
>   One mo' ribber to cross.
> Oh, you got Jesus, hold him fast,
>   One mo' ribber to cross.
> Oh, better love was nebber told,
>   One mo' ribber to cross.
> 'Tis stronger dan an iron band,
>   One mo' ribber to cross.
> 'Tis sweeter dan de honey comb,
>   One mo' ribber to cross.
> Oh, de good ole chariot passin' by,
>   One mo' ribber to cross.
> She jarred de earth an' shook de sky,
>   One mo' ribber to cross.
> I pray, good Lord, I shall be one,
>   One mo' ribber to cross.
> To get in de chariot an' trabble on,
>   One mo' ribber to cross.
> We're told dat de fore wheel run by love,
>   One mo' ribber to cross.
> We're told dat de hind wheel run by faith,
>   One mo' ribber to cross.
> I hope I'll get dere by an' bye,
>   One mo' ribber to cross.
> To jine de number in de sky,
>   One mo' ribber to cross.
> Oh, Jordan's Ribber am chilly an' cold,
>   One mo' ribber to cross.
> It chills de body, but not de soul,
>   One mo' ribber to cross.

A study of the Spirituals leads to the belief that the earlier ones were built upon the form so common to African songs, leading lines and response. It would be safe, I think, to say that the bulk of the Spirituals

PREFACE

are cast in this simple form. Among those following this simple structure, however, are some of the most beautiful of the slave songs. One
of these, whose beauty is unsurpassed, is *Swing Low, Sweet Chariot*,
which is constructed to be sung in the following manner:

Leader:	Swing low, sweet chariot,
Congregation:	Comin' for to carry me home.
Leader:	Swing low, sweet chariot,
Congregation:	Comin' for to carry me home.
Leader:	I look over Jordan, what do I see?
Congregation:	Comin' for to carry me home.
Leader:	A band of angels comin' after me,
Congregation:	Comin' for to carry me home.
Leader:	Swing low, sweet chariot,
	etc., etc., etc.

The solitary voice of the leader is answered by a sound like a rolling
sea. The effect produced is strangely moving.

But as the American Negro went a step beyond his original African
music in the development of melody and harmony, he also went a step
beyond in the development of form. The lead and response are still
retained, but the response is developed into a true chorus. In a number of the songs there are leads, a response and a chorus. In this
class of songs the chorus becomes the most important part, dominating
the whole song and coming first. Such a song is the well known "Steal
Away to Jesus." In this song the congregation begins with the chorus,
singing it in part harmony:

Steal away, steal away,
Steal away to Jesus.
Steal away, steal away home,
I ain't got long to stay here.

Then the leader alone or the congregation in unison:

My Lord He calls me,
He calls me by the thunder,
The trumpet sounds within-a my soul.

26

Then the response in part harmony:

> I ain't got long to stay here.

> Steal away, steal away,
>   etc., etc., etc.

This developed form is carried a degree farther in "Go Down Moses." Here the congregation opens with the powerful theme of the chorus, singing it in unison down to the last line, which is harmonized:

> Go down, Moses,
> 'Way down in Egypt land,
> Tell ole Pharaoh,
> Let my people go.

Then the leader:

> Thus saith the Lord, bold Moses said,

And the response:

> Let my people go.

Leader:

> If not I'll smite your first-born dead.

Response:

> Let my people go.

Chorus:

> Go down, Moses,
> Go down, Moses,
> 'Way down in Egypt land,
> Tell ole Pharaoh,
> Let my people go.
>   etc., etc., etc.

In a few of the songs this development is carried to a point where the form becomes almost purely choral. Examples of these more complex structures are, *Deep River,* and *Walk Together Children.*

PREFACE

I have said that the European concept of music, generally speaking, is melody and the African concept is rhythm. It is upon this point that most white people have difficulty with Negro music, the difficulty of getting the "swing" of it. White America has pretty well mastered this difficulty; and naturally, because the Negro has been beating these rhythms in its ears for three hundred years. But in Europe, in spite of the vogue of American popular music, based on these rhythms, the best bands are not able to play it satisfactorily. Of course, they play the notes correctly, but any American can at once detect that there is something lacking. The trouble is, they play the notes too correctly; and do not play what is not written down. There are few things more ludicrous—to an American—than the efforts of a European music hall artist to sing a jazz song. It is interesting, if not curious, that among white Americans those who have mastered these rhythms most completely are Jewish-Americans. Indeed, Jewish musicians and composers are they who have carried them to their highest development in written form.

In all authentic American Negro music the rhythms may be divided roughly into two classes—rhythms based on the swinging of head and body and rhythms based on the patting of hands and feet. Again, speaking roughly, the rhythms of the Spirituals fall in the first class and the rhythms of secular music in the second class. The "swing" of the Spirituals is an altogether subtle and elusive thing. It is subtle and elusive because it is in perfect union with the religious ecstasy that manifests itself in the swaying bodies of a whole congregation, swaying as if responding to the baton of some extremely sensitive conductor. So it is very difficult, if not impossible, to sing these songs sitting or standing coldly still, and at the same time capture the spontaneous "swing" which is of their very essence.

Carl Van Vechten writing in *Vanity Fair* about these songs declared it as his opinion that white singers cannot sing them, and that women, with few exceptions, should not attempt to sing them at all. Mr. Van Vechten made this statement in recognition of the element in the Spirituals without which their beauty of melody and harmony is lifeless. His statement also, I take it, has specific reference to the singing of these songs as solos on the concert stage. I agree that white singers are, naturally, prone to go to either of two extremes: to attempt to render a Spiritual as though it were a Brahms song, or to assume a ''Negro unctuousness'' that is obviously false, and painfully so. I think white singers, concert singers, *can* sing Spirituals— if they *feel* them. But to feel them it is necessary to know the truth about their origin and history, to get in touch with the association of ideas that surround them, and to realize something of what they have meant in the experiences of the people who created them. In a word, the capacity to *feel* these songs while singing them is more important than any amount of mere artistic technique. Singers who take the Spirituals as mere ''art'' songs and singers who make of them an exhibition of what is merely amusing or exotic are equally doomed to failure, so far as true interpretation is concerned. Mr. Van Vechten's opinion brings up the question of the rendition of these songs as concert solos not only by white but by colored singers. I have seen more than one colored singer floundering either in the ''art'' or the ''exhibition'' pit. The truth is, these songs, primarily created and constructed, as they were, for group singing, will always remain a high test for the individual artist. They are not concert material for the mediocre soloist. Through the genius and supreme artistry of Roland Hayes these songs undergo, we may say, a transfiguration. He takes them high above the earth and sheds over them shimmering silver of moonlight and flashes of the sun's gold; and we are transported as he sings. By a seemingly opposite method, through sheer simplicity, without any conscious attempt at artistic effort and by devoted adherence to the primitive traditions, Paul Robeson achieves substantially the same effect. These two singers, apparently so different, have the chief essential in common; they both feel the Spirituals deeply. Mr. Hayes, notwithstanding all his artistry, sings these songs with tears on his cheeks. Both these singers pull at the heart strings and moisten the eyes of their listeners.

We were discussing the ''swing'' of the Spirituals, and were saying how subtle and elusive a thing it was. It is the more subtle and elusive because there is a still further intricacy in the rhythms. The swaying of the body marks the regular beat or, better, surge, for it is something stronger than a beat, and is more or less, not precisely,

29

strict in time; but the Negro loves nothing better in his music than to play with the fundamental time beat. He will, as it were, take the fundamental beat and pound it out with his left hand, almost monotonously; while with his right hand he juggles it. It should be noted that even in the swaying of head and body the head marks the surge off in shorter waves than does the body. In listening to Negroes sing their own music it is often tantalizing and even exciting to watch a minute fraction of a beat balancing for a slight instant on the bar between two measures, and, when it seems almost too late, drop back into its own proper compartment. There is a close similarity between this singing and the beating of the big drum and the little drums by the African natives. In addition, there are the curious turns and twists and quavers and the intentional striking of certain notes just a shade off the key, with which the Negro loves to embellish his songs. These tendencies constitute a handicap that has baffled many of the recorders of this music. I doubt that it is possible with our present system of notation to make a fixed transcription of these peculiarities that would be absolutely true; for in their very nature they are not susceptible to fixation. Many of the transcriptions that have been made are far from the true manner and spirit of singing the Spirituals. I have gone thus far into the difficulties connected with singing the Spirituals in order that those who are interested in these songs may have a fuller understanding of just what they are. It is not necessary to say that the lack of complete mastery of all these difficulties is not at all fatal to deriving pleasure from singing Spirituals. A group does not have to be able to sing with the fervor and abandon of a Negro congregation to enjoy them. Nor does one have to be a Hayes or a Robeson to give others an idea of their beauty and power.

Going back again, the rhythms of Negro secular music, roughly speaking, fall in the class based on the patting of hands and feet. It can easily be seen that this distinction between the Spirituals and Negro secular music is, in a large way, that of different physical responses to differing sets of emotions. Religious ecstasy fittingly manifests itself in swaying heads and bodies; the emotions that call for hand and foot patting are pleasure, humor, hilarity, love, just the joy of being alive. In this class of his music, as in the Spirituals,

PREFACE

the Negro is true to the characteristic of playing with the fundamental beat; if anything, more so. What is largely psychological manifestation in the Spirituals becomes physical response in the secular music. In this music the fundamental beat is chiefly maintained by the patting of one foot, while the hands clap out intricate and varying rhythmic patterns. It should be understood that the foot is not marking straight time, but what Negroes call "stop time," or what the books have no better definition for than "syncopation." The strong accent or down beat is never lost, but is playfully bandied from hand to foot and from foot to hand.

I wish to point out here that the rhapsodical hand clapping connected with singing the Spirituals—except in the "ring shout" songs, of which I shall speak later—is not to be confused with the hand clapping to dance-time music. Recently another Negro dance has swept the country. It was introduced to New York by Messrs. Miller and Lyles in their musical comedy, *Runnin' Wild*. And at present white people everywhere, in the cabarets, on the ball floor and at home count it an accomplishment to be able to "do the Charleston." When Miller and Lyles introduced the dance in their play they did not depend wholly on the orchestra—an extraordinary jazz band—for the accompaniment, but had the major part of the chorus supplement it with hand and foot patting. The effect was electrical and contagious. It was the best demonstration of beating out complex rhythms I have ever witnessed; and, I do not believe New York ever before witnessed anything of just its sort.

It would be interesting to know how many peoples there are other than the Negro in America and Africa, if there are any, who innately beat out these complex and extremely intricate rhythms with their hands and feet. The Spanish people do something of the kind in their castanet dances; but, as has already been shown, this is probably the result of African influence. At any rate, this innate characteristic of the Negro in America is the genesis and foundation of our national popular medium for musical expression.

The temptations for these digressions are almost irresistible. At this point the writer could go far along the line of discussing the origin of Negro secular music and its development until it was finally

31

PREFACE

taken over and made "American popular music." It would be easy also to stray along a parallel line, and note how Negro dances have kept step with Negro secular music, and how from their inglorious beginnings they have advanced until they have been recognized and accepted by the stage and by "society." And this merely to pave the way for another slight digression. And, yet, we can hardly discuss the question of Negro rhythms and "swing" without paying some attention to still another class of songs—the work songs.

With regard to rhythm and "swing" the work songs do not fall into the classification with either the Spirituals or the dance-time songs. The "swing" of these songs is governed by the rhythmic motions made by a gang of men at labor. It may be the motions made in swinging a pick on the road or a hammer on the rock pile, or in loading cotton on the levée. Some of the finest examples of these songs are those originated by the convicts at work in the chain gang. One of these is the poignantly beautiful "Water Boy" frequently sung by Roland Hayes. All the men sing and move together as they swing their picks or rock-breaking hammers. They move like a ballet; not a ballet of cavorting legs and pirouetting feet, but a ballet of bending backs and quivering muscles. It is all in rhythm but a rhythm impossible to set down. There is always a leader and he sets the pace. A phrase is sung while the shining hammers are being lifted. It is cut off suddenly as the hammers begin to descend and gives place to a prolonged grunt which becomes explosive at the impact of the blow. Each phrase of the song is independent, apparently obeying no law of time. After each impact the hammers lie still and there is silence. As they begin to rise again the next phrase of the song is sung; and so on. Just how long the hammers will be allowed to rest cannot be determined; nor, since the movements are not governed by strict time, can any exact explanation be given as to why they all begin to rise simultaneously. There are variations that violate the obvious laws of rhythm, but over it all can be discerned a superior rhythmic law. A fine illustration of what I have been trying to explain was given by Paul Robeson in his rendition of the convict song in "The Emperor Jones."

Brief mention must be made of another class of Negro songs. This

32

is a remnant of songs allied to the Spirituals but which cannot be strictly classified with them. They are the ''shout songs.'' These songs are not true spirituals nor even truly religious; in fact, they are not actually songs. They might be termed quasi-religious or semi-barbaric music. They once were used, and still are in a far less degree, in religious gatherings, but neither musically nor in the manner of their use do they fall in the category of the Spirituals. This term ''shout songs'' has no reference to the loud, jubilant Spirituals, which are often so termed by writers on Negro music; it has reference to the songs or, better, the chants used to accompany the ''ring shout.'' The ''ring shout,'' in truth, is nothing more or less than the survival of a primitive African dance, which in quite an understandable way attached itself in the early days to the Negro's Christian worship. I can remember seeing this dance many times when I was a boy. A space is cleared by moving the benches, and the men and women arrange themselves, generally alternately, in a ring, their bodies quite close. The music starts and the ring begins to move. Around it goes, at first slowly, then with quickening pace. Around and around it moves on shuffling feet that do not leave the floor, one foot beating with the heel a decided accent in strict two-four time. The music is supplemented by the clapping of hands. As the ring goes around it begins to take on signs of frenzy. The music, starting, perhaps, with a Spiritual, becomes a wild, monotonous chant. The same musical phrase is repeated over and over one, two, three, four, five hours. The words become a repetition of an incoherent cry. The very monotony of sound and motion produces an ecstatic state. Women, screaming, fall to the ground prone and quivering. Men, exhausted, drop out of the shout. But the ring closes up and moves around and around.

I remember, too, that even then the ''ring shout'' was looked upon as a very questionable form of worship. It was distinctly frowned upon by a great many colored people. Indeed, I do not recall ever seeing a ''ring shout'' except *after* the regular services. Almost whispered invitations would go around, ''Stay after church; there's going to be a 'ring shout.' '' The more educated ministers and members, as fast as they were able to brave the primitive element in the churches, placed a ban on the ''ring shout.'' The ''shout,'' however, was never universal. The best information that I have been able to gather indicates that it was most general in the Atlantic and Gulf coastal regions of the south-eastern states. Today it is rarely seen. It has not quite, but has almost disappeared. In parts of Louisiana, and in some parts of the West Indies and South America, or, in other words, where the Negro came under the influence and jurisdiction of the Catholic Church and the Church of England this dance long persisted outside of the church and Christian religion. There it retained its primitive social and ceremonial significance and was practiced with more or less frankness. Two reasons may be advanced to cover these two facts: under the Catholic Church and the Church of England the Negro, practically, never had any place of worship of his own, and, of course, he would never have been allowed to introduce such a practice as the "ring shout," even under a religious guise, into those churches; it is also in a large measure true that the Negro in those localities has never accepted the Christian religion in the sense and degree in which it was accepted by the Negro of the South; there his acceptance was more a matter of outward conformity, and he clung more tenaciously to his African cultural and religious ideas. This survival of an African ceremony has been outlawed in the United States and cannot be seen except in some backward churches of a backward community. But in parts of the West Indies and South America it is still quite frankly practiced as a social function. The Negroes that live along the eastern fringe of Venezuela dance every Saturday. I have often heard their chants and the drums throbbing until far into the night. I was in Haiti several years ago and I learned that the "Saturday night dance," which had been the custom there, too, had been interdicted in the larger cities by the American Occupation authorities. However, the people were still allowed to dance in the rural districts and on holidays. On one national holiday in a small village I saw them dance under a thatched pavilion in the little public square. It was the same thing I had seen in my childhood in a small church in Florida. The formation of the dancers was the same, the shuffling motion was the same, the monotonous, incoherent chant sounded the same, although these folk spoke an unfamiliar language. The only differences I noted were: it was not in a church,

34

there was great gaiety instead of religious frenzy, and the beating drums—real African drums.

I refer again to Mr. Van Vechten's interesting article. In it he said, "Negro folksongs differ from the folksongs of most other races through the fact that they are sung in harmony." I am glad to have this confirmation of my own opinion. I have long thought that the harmonization of the Spirituals by the folk group in singing them was distinctive of them among the folksongs of the world. My speculation was with regard to how many other groups of folksongs there were that were harmonized spontaneously in the singing. The fact that the Spirituals were sung in harmony has always seemed natural to me, because Negroes harmonize instinctively. What about the traditional reputation of Negroes as singers; upon what is it really founded? The common idea is that it is founded upon the quality of their voices. It is not. The voices of Negroes, when untrained, are often overloud, perhaps rather blatant, sometimes even a bit strident; but they are *never discordant*. In harmony they take on an orchestra-like timbre. The popular credit given to Negroes as singers is given, maybe unconsciously, because of their ability to harmonize, and not because of the quality of their voices. When the folks at the "big house" sat on the verandah and heard the singing floating up through the summer night from the "quarters" they were enchanted; and it is likely they did not realize that the enchantment was wrought chiefly through the effect produced by harmonizing and not by the voices as voices.

Pick up four colored boys or young men anywhere and the chances are ninety out of a hundred that you have a quartet. Let one of them sing the melody and the others will naturally find the parts. Indeed, it may be said that all male Negro youth of the United States is divided into quartets. When I was a very small boy one of my greatest pleasures was going to concerts and hearing the crack quartets made up of waiters in the Jacksonville hotels sing. Each of the big Florida resort hotels boasted at least two quartets, a first and a second. When I was fifteen and my brother was thirteen we were singing in a quartet which competed with other quartets. In the days when such a thing as a white barber was unknown in the South, every barber shop had its quartet, and the men spent their leisure time playing on the guitar —not banjo, mind you—and "harmonizing." I have witnessed some of these explorations in the field of harmony and the scenes of hilarity and back-slapping when a new and peculiarly rich chord was discovered. There would be demands for repetitions, and cries of "Hold it! Hold it!" until it was firmly mastered. And well it was, for some of these chords were so new and strange for voices that, like Sullivan's *Lost Chord,* they would never have been found again except for the celerity with which they were recaptured. In this way was born the famous but much abused "barber-shop chord."

It may sound like an extravagant claim, but it is, nevertheless a fact that the "barber-shop chord" is the foundation of the close harmony method adopted by American musicians in making arrangements for male voices. I do not think English musicians have yet used this method of arranging to any great extent. "Barber-shop harmonies" gave a tremendous vogue to male quartet singing, first on the minstrel stage, then in vaudeville; and soon white young men, wherever four or more were gathered together, tried themselves at "harmonizing." The vogue somewhat declined because the old "barber-shop chord" was so overdone that it became almost taboo. But the male quartet is still one of the main features of colored musical shows. These modern quartets avoid the stereotyped chords of twenty, thirty and forty years ago, but the chief charm of their singing still lies in the closeness of the harmony. No one who heard *Shuffle Along,* can forget the singing of *The Four Harmony Kings.*

Among the early collectors of the Spirituals there was some doubt as to whether they were sung in harmony. This confusion may have been due in part to the fact that in the Spirituals the Negro makes such frequent use of unison harmony. The leading lines are always sung by a single voice or in unison harmony, and many of the refrains or choruses are sung in unison harmony down to the last phrase, and then in part harmony. The chorus of *Go Down Moses* is an example. In *Slave Songs of the United States,* published in 1867, Mr. Allen, one of the editors, in accounting for the fact that only the melodies of the songs in the collection were printed, said in his preface:

PREFACE

"There is no singing in parts, as we understand it, and yet no two seem to be singing the same thing; the leading singer starts the words of each verse, often improvising, and others, who 'base' him, as it is called, strike in with the refrain or even join in the solo when the words are familiar. When the 'base' begins the leader often stops, leaving the rest of the words to be guessed at, or it may be they are taken up by one of the other singers. And the 'basers' themselves seem to follow their own whims, beginning where they please, striking an octave above or below (in case they have pitched the tune too high), or hitting some other note that chords, so as to produce the effect of a marvelous complication and variety and yet with the most perfect time and rarely with any discord. And what makes it all the harder to unravel a thread of melody out of this strange network is that, like birds, they seem not infrequently to strike sounds that cannot be precisely represented by the gamut and abound in 'slides' from one note to another and turns and cadences not in articulated notes."

Mr. Allen's opinion that the songs were not harmonized is explained when he says, "There is no singing in parts, as we understand it." And no one can blame him for not attempting to do more than transcribe the melodies. If Mr. Allen were writing today, when America is so familiar with the bizarre Negro harmonies, he would recognize that the Spirituals were harmonized and he would try to transcribe the harmonies. What he heard was the primitive and spontaneous group singing of the Spirituals, and his description of it is, perhaps, as good as can be given. It might also be noted that it is an excellent description of the most modern American form of instrumentation, —a form that most people think of as a brand new invention.

The songs collected in this book have been arranged for solo voice, but in the piano accompaniments the arrangers have sincerely striven to give the characteristic harmonies that would be used in spontaneous group singing. Of course, these harmonies are not fixed. A group or congregation singing spontaneously might never use precisely the same harmonies twice; however, Mr. Rosamond Johnson and Mr. Brown have shown great fidelity to what is characteristic. The ordinary four-part harmonies can, without difficulty, be picked out from the accompaniments to most of the songs, but what the arrangers

37

PREFACE

had principally in mind was to have the instrumentation approach the effect of the singing group in action.

What can be said about the poetry of the texts of the Spirituals? Naturally, not so much as can be said about the music. In the use of the English language both the bards and the group worked under limitations that might appear to be hopeless. Many of the lines are less than trite, and irrelevant repetition often becomes tiresome. They are often saved alone by their naïveté. And yet there is poetry, and a surprising deal of it in the Spirituals. There is more than ought to be reasonably expected from a forcedly ignorant people working in an absolutely alien language. Hebraic paraphrases are frequent. These are accounted for by the fact that the Bible was the chief source of material for the lines of these songs.

> Upon de mountain Jehovah spoke,
> Out-a his mouth came fi-ar and smoke.

But in these paraphrases we have something that is not exactly paraphrase; there is a change of, I dare to say it, style; something Hebrew—austerity—is lessened, and something Negro—charm—is injected. Examples could be multiplied:

> I wrastled wid Satan, I wrastled wid sin
> Stepped over hell, an' come back agin.

> Isaiah mounted on de wheel of time
> Spoke to God A-mighty 'way down de line.

> O hear dat lumberin' thunder
> A-roll f'om door to door,
> A-callin' de people home to God,
> Dey'll git home bime-by.

> O see dat forkéd lightenin'
> A-jump f'om cloud to cloud,
> A-pickin' up God's chillun
> Dey'll git home bime-by.

Here are lines suggestive of what may be found in the Psalms; and yet how distinctively different:

38

PREFACE

Sinner, sinner, you better pray,
Looks like my Lord a-comin' in de sky.
Or yo' soul be los' on de jedgment day,
Looks like my Lord a-comin' in de sky.

O little did I think he was so nigh,
Looks like my Lord a-comin' in de sky.
He spoke an' he made me laugh and cry,
Looks like my Lord a-comin' in de sky.

When I was a monah jes like you,
Looks like my Lord a-comin' in de sky.
My head got wet wid de midnight dew,
Looks like my Lord a-comin' in de sky.

My head got wet wid de midnight dew,
Looks like my Lord a-comin' in de sky.
De mornin' star was a witness too,
Looks like my Lord a-comin' in de sky.

Many of the stories and scenes in the Bible gave the Negro bards great play for their powers of graphic description. The stories are always dramatic and the pictures vivid and gorgeously colored. The style, in contradiction of the general idea of Negro diffuseness, is concise and condensed. It might be said of them that every line is a picture. The following illustrative lines are taken from a Spiritual derived from John's vision on Patmos:

Yes, the book of Revelations will be brought forth dat day,
An' ev'ry leaf unfolded, the book of the seven seals.

An' I went down to Egypt, I camped upon de groun'
At de soundin' of de trumpet de Holy Ghost came down.

An' when de seals were opened, the voice said, "Come an' see,"
I went an' stood a-lookin to see de mystery.

The red horse came a-gallopin', an' de black horse he came too,
An' de pale horse he came down de road, an' stole my father away.

An' den I see ole Satan, an' dey bound him wid a chain,
An' dey put him in de fi-ar, an' I see de smoke arise.

39

PREFACE

Dey bound him in de fi-ar, where he wanted to take my soul,
Ole Satan gnashed his teeth and howled, he missed po' sinner man's soul.

Den I see de dead arisin', an' stan' before de Lamb
An' de wicked call on de mountains to hide dem f'om His face.

An' den I see de Christians standin' on God's right hand,
A shoutin' "Hallelujah!" singing praises to de Lamb.

Sometimes these biblical incidents are resolved into lyrical gems.
I quote a stanza from the song about Jacob wrestling with the angel,
found in Colonel Thomas Wentworth Higginson's book:

> O wrestlin' Jacob, Jacob day's a-breakin',
> I will not let thee go!
> O wrestlin' Jacob, Jacob day's a-breakin',
> He will not let me go!
> O, I hold my brudder wid a tremblin' hand;
> I would not let him go!
> I hold my sister wid a tremblin' hand;
> I would not let her go!

But see what these Negro bards have done with the story of the
crucifixion. They have not merely rehearsed it as it is given in the
gospels: they have fused into it their very own pathos:

> Dey crucified my Lord,
> An' He never said a mumblin' word.
> Dey crucified my Lord,
> An' he never said a mumblin' word,
> Not a word—not a word—not a word.
>
> Dey nailed Him to de tree,
> An' He never said a mumblin' word.
> Dey nailed Him to de tree,
> An' He never said a mumblin' word,
> Not a word—not a word—not a word.
>
> Dey pierced Him in de side,
> An' He never said a mumblin' word.
> Dey pierced Him in de side,

40

PREFACE

An' He never said a mumblin' word,
Not a word—not a word—not a word.

De blood came twinklin' down,
  An' He never said a mumblin' word.
De blood came twinklin' down,
  An' He never said a mumblin' word,
Not a word—not a word—not a word.

He bowed His head an' died,
  An' He never said a mumblin' word.
He bowed His head and died,
  An' He never said a mumblin' word,
Not a word—not a word—not a word.

The word "twinklin' " in the fourth stanza is a Negro pronunciation of the word "trinkling." But in this way what a magical poetic phrase was stumbled upon, "The blood came twinkling down."

In rare instances a touch of the irrepressible Negro humor creeps in:

Ev'ybody talkin' 'bout heaben ain' gwine der.

Sister, you better mind how you walk on de cross,
Yo' foot might slip an' yo' soul git los'.

De devil is a liar an' a conjurer too,
Ef you don't look out he'll conjure you.

Much, too, of the poetry of the Spirituals is the Negro's innate expression of his own emotions and experiences; and out of these he drew some piercing lyrical cries:

Sometimes I feel like a motherless child,
Sometimes I feel like a motherless child,
Sometimes I feel like a motherless child,
A long ways from home.

Or in the opposite mood:

Sometimes I feel like an eagle in de air
Some-a dese mornin's bright an' fair
I'm goin' to lay down my heavy load;
Goin' to spread my wings an' cleave de air.

41

PREFACE

You may bury me in de east,
You may bury me in de west,
But I'll hear de trumpet sound
In-a dat mornin'.

Occasionally we are startled by a flash of poetry of pure beauty; of poetry not circumscribed by individual conditions, but coming out of the experiences of humanity. I quote, in concluding these examples, again from Colonel Higginson's book:

I know moon-rise, I know star-rise,
  I lay dis body down.
I walk in de moonlight, I walk in de starlight,
  To lay dis body down.
I walk in de graveyard, I walk throo de graveyard,
  To lay dis body down.
I lie in de grave an' stretch out my arms,
  I lay dis body down.
I go to de jedgment in de evenin' of de day
  When I lay dis body down,
An' my soul an' your soul will meet in de day
  When I lay dis body down.

Regarding the line, "I lie in de grave an' stretch out my arms," Colonel Higginson wrote: "Never, it seems to me, since man first lived and suffered, was his infinite longing for peace uttered more plaintively than in that line."

Something should be said to give a general idea about the "language" in which these songs were written. Negro dialect in America is the result of the effort of the slave to establish a medium of communication between himself and his master. This he did by dropping his original language, and formulating a phonologically and grammatically simplified English; that is, an English in which the harsh and difficult sounds were elided, and the secondary moods and tenses were eliminated. This dialect served not only as a means of communication between slave and master but also between slave and slave; so the original African languages became absolutely lost. The dialect spoken in the sea islands off the coast of Georgia and South Carolina remains

42

PREFACE

closer to African form than the dialect of any other section, and still contains some African words. It is, at any rate, farther from English than the speech of American Negroes anywhere else. But it is remarkable how few words of known African origin there are in the Negro dialect generally spoken throughout the United States.

Negro dialect, in substantially its present form, has been used in the United States for the past two centuries. In the South all white people, men, women and children, understand the dialect without any shadow of difficulty. Indeed, the English spoken by the whites does not differ, in some respects, from the dialect; so great has been the influence of this soft, indolent speech of the Negro. Nevertheless, Negro dialect presents some difficulties to white people who have never lived in the South, when they attempt to reproduce it in speech or in song. Of course, it is not necessary to be an expert in Negro dialect to sing the Spirituals, but most of them lose in charm when they are sung in straight English. For example, it would be next to sacrilege to render:

"What kinda shoes you gwine to weah?"

by:

"What kind of shoes are you going to wear?"

An error that confuses many persons is the idea that Negro dialect is uniform and fixed. The idioms and pronunciation of the dialect vary in different sections of the South. A Negro of the uplands of Georgia does not speak the identical dialect of his brother of the islands off the coast of the state, and would have a hard time understanding him. Nor is the generally spoken Negro dialect the fixed thing it is made to be on the printed page. It is variable and fluid. Not even in the dialect of any particular section is a given word always pronounced the same. It may vary slightly in the next breath in the mouth of the same speaker. How a word is pronounced is governed by the preceding and following sounds. Sometimes the combination permits of a liaison so close that to the uninitiated the sound of the word is almost lost.

To illustrate: If one dialect-speaking Negro asks another, "Is dat all you got to say?" the answer in the affirmative would be "Das all."

43

PREFACE

The invariable practice on the printed page is to represent "that" by "dat" and, logically ,"that's" by "dat's." But the harsh "ts" sound is displeasing to the Negro ear, as well as troublesome to the Negro tongue, so it is softened into "das."

Negro dialect is for many people made unintelligible on the printed page by the absurd practice of devising a clumsy, outlandish, so-called phonetic spelling for words in a dialect story or poem when the regular English spelling represents the very same sound. Paul Laurence Dunbar did a great deal to reform the writing down of dialect, but since it is more a matter of ear than of rules those who are not intimately familiar with the sounds continue to make the same blunders.

Since the understanding of the Spirituals and the pleasure of singing them are increased by a knowledge of the dialect in which the texts were composed, a suggestion or two about it will not be out of place. The first thing to remember is that the dialect is fundamentally English. An American from any part of the United States or an Englishman can, with not more than slight difficulty, understand it when it is spoken. The trouble comes in trying to get it from the printed page. There are some idioms that may be strange, but they are few. The next thing to remember is that the pronunciation of the dialect is the result of the elision by the Negro, as far as possible, of all troublesome consonants and sound combinations.

> Thus: "th" as in "that" or "than" becomes "d"
> "th" as in "thick" or "thin" becomes "t"

This rule holds good at the end as well as at the beginning of words and syllables. So we have "dat" and "der" or "dar," and "tick" and "tin," and "wid" and "det" (for death). Indeed, the Negro tries to elide the "h" whenever it is in combination with another consonant. There is always the tendency to suppress the "r," except when it is the initial letter of the syllable. The "g" in "ing" endings is generally dropped or smothered, and the sound resembles the final French "m" and "n." "A," "e" and "u," between two consonants in an unaccented syllable, are uniformly rendered by the sound of "u" in "but." The sound is sometimes broadened almost to the "a" in

44

PREFACE

"father." This is not an inflexible rule, but it especially holds true with regard to final syllables. (It may be remembered that this same tendency, in a less degree, is true of correct English.) Examples: The word "never" may be heard either as "nevuh" or as "nevah." This word is often playfully emphasized by a strong accent on the last syllable, "neváh." In the word "better" the first "e" has the usual short "e" sound, and the second "e" follows the above rule. Thus we have "bettuh" or "bettah." The word "to" is always pronounced "tuh." The "or" and "our" combinations are generally sounded "oh," as "do'" or "doh" for "door," and "monuh" or "monah" for "mourner." This dialect word, by the way, does not signify one undergoing grief, but one undergoing repentance for sins.

Perhaps the most common mistake made in imitating Negro dialect is in giving to "de," the dialect for "the," the unvarying pronunciation of "dee." It is pronounced "dee" when it precedes words beginning with a vowel sound, and "duh" before those beginning with a consonant sound. In this it follows the rule for the article "the."

The statement that the Negro dialect generally spoken in the United States is fundamentally English brings up a curious fact regarding the effort of a smaller group of Negro slaves to create a medium of communication between themselves and their masters. This fact is the more apropos because this smaller group also created a rich body of folksongs. In what was the Territory of Louisiana the language was French. The Negro slaves of the Territory, in establishing a medium of communication, instead of forming a dialect of the French language, created a distinct language. This language is known as Creole. Creole is an Africanized French, but it is neither African nor French. It is a language in itself. The French-speaking person cannot, with the exception of some words, understand it unless he learns it. Creole is a distinct language, scientifically constructed and logical in its grammatical arrangement. It is a graphic and expressive language, and is, in some respects, superior to French.

For a reason I cannot give, wherever there was a Negro population the French language in the French-American colonial settlements divided itself into two branches—French and Creole. This is true of Louisiana, of Martinique, of Guadaloupe and of Haiti. No such thing

45

happened with the Spanish language. Negroes in the Spanish-American countries speak Spanish.

In setting down the words of the songs here included I have endeavored to keep them as true to the original dialect as is compatible with a more or less ready recognition of what the words really are. When a dialect spelling would puzzle and confuse the reader and actually throw him off, the regular English spelling has been followed. This, for example, was the practice followed in writing the word "sword" in the song *Singing With a Sword in My Hand*. The spelling "sode" or "soad" would have been positively misleading. I am sure this method is preferable to an attempt to indicate by phonetic spelling all the exact sounds of Negro dialect. I have seen "unuthuh" printed for "another." The ordinary pronunciation of the regular English spelling is so close to the dialect that the difference does not warrant such a task in deciphering being placed upon the reader. It will be noticed that in some of the songs the exaggerated form of dialect would not be fitting; in such songs I have kept the dialect forms down to the minimum. With a general idea of the principles of the dialect the reader or singer may give even Negro songs written in straight English the proper color.

This book is dedicated to those through whose efforts these songs have been collected, preserved and given to the world. It is a fitting, if inadequate, tribute; for it was wholly within the possibilities for these songs to be virtually lost. The people who created them were not capable of recording them, and the conditions out of which this music sprang and by which it was nourished have almost passed away. Without the direct effort on the part of those to whom I offer this slight tribute, the Spirituals would probably have fallen into disuse and finally disappeared. This probability is increased by the fact that they passed through a period following Emancipation when the front ranks of the colored people themselves would have been willing and even glad to let them die.

The first efforts towards the preservation of this music were made by the pioneer collectors who worked within the decade following the Civil War. These collectors, either through curiosity or as a matter of research, or because they were impressed by the unique beauty of the Spirituals, set down on paper the words and melodies. All of them were more or less successful in getting the melodies down correctly, but none of these pioneers even attempted to set down the anarchic harmonies which they heard. In fact, they had no classification for these sounds or even comprehension of them as harmonies. These pioneers were none of them exceptionally trained, but on this point they were not one whit behind the most advanced thought in American music of their day. Some of these early collectors contented themselves with jotting down simply the melodies and words, and publishing their collections in that form. Others harmonized the melodies. These harmonized arrangements, however, had little or no relation to the original harmonies or the manner of singing them by the group. They were, generally, straight four-part arrangements set down in strict accordance with the standard rules of thorough-bass. Nevertheless, except for the work of these pioneer collectors, done mostly as a labor of love, the number of the Spirituals recorded and preserved would have been only a small fraction of what it is.

The credit for the first introduction of the Spirituals to the American public and the world belongs to Fisk University. It was the famous Fisk Jubilee Singers that first made this country and Europe conscious of the beauty of these songs. The story of the struggles and successes of the Jubilee Singers, as told in the Fisk Collection of the Spirituals, reads like a romance. The first impetus upward was given them in New York under the powerful patronage of Henry Ward Beecher. With far-reaching wisdom Fisk University devoted itself to the careful collection and recording of the Spirituals, and so the work of the earlier collectors was broadened and improved upon. The work of Fisk University was quickly followed up by Hampton; Calhoun School, in Alabama; Atlanta University; Tuskegee Institute, and other schools in the South. These schools have for two generations been nurseries and homes for these songs.

Within the past ten or twelve years thorough musicians have undertaken a study of this music; a scientific study of it as folk music and an evaluation of its sociological as well as its musical importance. Chief among these is H. E. Krehbiel, more than thirty years music critic on the New York Tribune. For many years Mr. Krehbiel made a study of Negro music, and gathered a vast amount of data. In 1914 he published his *Afro-American Folksongs,* which has already been referred to here. Shortly afterwards an excellent and sound book on the subject, *Folk Songs of the American Negro,* was published by Professor John W. Work of Fisk University. Natalie Curtis Burlin issued *The Hampton Series—Negro Folk-Songs,* in four parts containing the results of her investigations and studies at Hampton aided by phonograph records. Maud Cuney Hare of Boston contributed to the sum of historical and scientific knowledge regarding Negro music. A number of foreign musicians and observers, mostly Germans, have written on the same theme.

Today the Spirituals have a vogue. They are beyond the place where the public might hear them only through the quartets of Fisk or Hampton or Atlanta or Tuskegee. Today the public buys the Spirituals, takes them home and plays and sings them. This has been brought about because the songs have been put into a form that makes them available for singers and music lovers. The principal factor in reaching this stage has been H. T. Burleigh, the eminent colored musician and composer. Mr. Burleigh was the pioneer in making arrangements for the Spirituals that widened their appeal and extended their use to singers and the general musical public. Along with Mr. Burleigh and following him was a group of talented colored composers working to the same end: Nathaniel Dett, Carl Diton, J. Rosamond Johnson and N. Clark Smith. The vogue of the Spirituals was added to by the publishing of twenty-four piano arrangements of Spirituals by Coleridge-Taylor. Clarence Cameron White of Boston published a number of arrangements for violin and piano. There were others who aided greatly by organizing choruses and teaching them to sing these songs; foremost among whom were Mrs. Azalia Hackley, Mrs. Daisy Tapley and William C. Elkins. The latest impulse given to the spread of the Spirituals has come within the last year or two through their presentation to the public by colored singers on the concert stage. The superlatively fine rendition of these songs by Roland Hayes, Paul Robeson, Miss Marian Anderson, and Julius Bledsoe has brought them to their highest point of celebrity and placed the classic stamp upon them. Today it is appropriate for any artist, however great, to program one or a group of these Spirituals.

A number of white persons aided in securing the general recognition which the Spirituals now enjoy. Several white musicians have made excellent arrangements for some of these songs. David Mannes, long interested in Negro music, was instrumental together with Mrs. Natalie Curtis Burlin, Mr. Elbridge Adams and others in founding a colored music school settlement in the Harlem section of New York City. Clement Wood, the poet, has for several years given lectures on the Spirituals, illustrated by voice and at the piano. Carl Van Vechten, whom I have quoted, has made a study of Negro music and has written a number of articles on the subject. But the present regard in which this Negro music is held is due overwhelmingly to the work of Negro composers, musicians and singers. It was through the work of these Negro artists that the colored people themselves were stirred to a realization of the true value of the Spirituals; and that result is more responsible for the new life which pulses through this music than any other single cause. I have said that these songs passed through a period when the front ranks of the Negro race would have been willing to let them die. Immediately following Emancipation those ranks revolted against everything connected with slavery, and among those things were the Spirituals. It became a sign of not being progressive or educated to sing them. This was a natural reaction, but, nevertheless, a sadly foolish one. It was left for the older generation to keep them alive by singing them at prayer meetings, class meetings, experience meetings and revivals, while the new choir with the organ and books of idiotic anthems held sway on Sundays. At this period gospel hymn-book agents reaped a harvest among colored churches in the South. Today this is all changed. There is hardly a choir among the largest and richest colored churches that does not make a specialty of singing the Spirituals. This re-awakening of the Negro to the value and beauty of the Spirituals was the beginning of an entirely new phase of race consciousness. It marked a change in the attitude of the Negro himself toward his own art material; the turning of his gaze inward upon his own cultural resources. Neglect and ashamedness gave place to study and pride. All the other artistic activities of the Negro have been influenced.

There is also a change of attitude going on with regard to the Negro. The country may not yet be conscious of it, for it is only in the beginning. It is, nevertheless, momentous. America is beginning to see the Negro in a new light, or, rather, to see something new in the Negro. It is beginning to see in him the divine spark which may glow merely for the fanning. And so a colored man is soloist for the Boston Symphony Orchestra and the Philharmonic; a colored woman is soloist for the Philadelphia Symphony Orchestra and the Philharmonic; colored singers draw concert goers of the highest class; Negro poets and writers find entrée to all the most important magazines; Negro authors have their books accepted and put out by the leading publishers. And this change of attitude with regard to the Negro which is taking place is directly related to the Negro's change of attitude with regard to himself. It is new, and it is tremendously significant.

The collection here presented is not definitive, but we have striven to make it representative of this whole field of music, to give examples of every variety of Spiritual. There is still enough material new and old for another book like this, and, perhaps, even for another.

In the arrangements, Mr. Rosamond Johnson and Mr. Brown have been true not only to the best traditions of the melodies but also to form. No changes have been made in the form of songs. The only development has been in harmonizations, and these harmonizations have been kept true in character. And so an old-time Negro singer could sing any of the songs through without encountering any innovations that would interrupt him or throw him off. They have not been cut up or "opera-ated" upon. The arrangers have endeavored above all else to retain their primitive "swing."

This collection is offered with the hope that it will further endear these songs to those who love Spirituals, and will awaken an interest in many others.

GO DOWN MOSES

Arranged by J. Rosamond Johnson

To Walter Damrosch

53

HEAV'N BOUN' SOLDIER

Arranged by J. Rosamond Johnson

To Julius Rosenwald

Hold out yo' light you heav'n boun' sol-dier, Hold out yo' light you heav'n boun' sol-dier, Hold out yo' light you heav'n boun' sol-dier, Let yo' light shine a-roun' de world.

O, dea - con can't yo' hold out yo' light, O, dea - con can't yo' hold out yo' light,
O, preach-er can't yo' hold out yo' light, O, preach-er can't yo' hold out yo' light,

O, dea - con can't yo' hold out yo' light, Let yo' light shine a - roun' de world.
O, preach-er can't yo' hold out yo' light, Let yo' light shine a - roun' de world.

Hold out yo' light, You heav'n boun' sol-dier, Hold out yo' light, yo' heav'n boun' sol-dier,

Repeat Leads ad lib. *Last time*

Hold out yo' light, You heav'n boun' sol-dier, Let yo' light shine a-roun' de world. world.

JOSHUA FIT DE BATTLE OB JERICO

Arranged by Lawrence Brown

To Paul and Eslanda Robeson

Josh - ua! At de bat - tle ob Jer - ʼr - co, Up to de walls, ob

Jer - i - co. He marched with spear in hanʼ "Go blow dem ram hornsʼ,

Josh - u - a cried, "Kase de bat - tle am in my hanʼ." Den deʼ

lamʼ ram sheep horns be - gin to blow, trum-pets be - gin to sounʼ,

57

58

WE AM CLIM'IN' JACOB'S LADDER

Arranged by J. Rosamond Johnson

To "Ma" White

DIDN'T OLD PHARAOH GET LOS'?

Arranged by J. Rosamond Johnson

To Azalia Hackley

EXTRA VERSES

(Quite often several verses are sung before returning to the chorus)

3. De Lord said unto Moses—
   "Go unto Pharaoh now,
   For I have hardened Pharaoh's heart,
   To me he will not bow."
   Cho.—Didn't old Pharaoh get los', etc.

4. Den Moses an' Aaron,
   To Pharaoh did go,
   "Thus says de God of Israel,
   Let my people go."
   Cho.—Didn't, etc.

5. Old Pharaoh said, "Who is de Lord
   Dat I should him obey?"
   "His name it is Jehovah,
   For he hears his people pray."
   Cho.—Didn't, etc.

6. Hark! hear de children murmur,
   Dey cry aloud for bread,
   Down came de hidden manna,
   De hungry soldiers fed.
   Cho.—Didn't, etc.

7. Den Moses numbered Israel,
   Through all de land abroad,
   Sayin', "Children, do not murmur,
   But hear de word of God."
   Cho.—Didn't, etc.

8. Den Moses said to Israel,
   As dey stood along de Shore
   "Yo' enemies you see today,
   You'll never see no more."
   Cho.—Didn't, etc.

9. Den down came raging Pharaoh,
   Dat you may plainly see,
   Old Pharaoh an' his host
   Got los' in de Red Sea.
   Cho.—Didn't, etc.

10. Den men an' women an' children
    To Moses dey did flock;
    Dey cried aloud for water,
    An' Moses smote de rock.
    Cho.—Didn't, etc.

11. An' de Lord spoke to Moses,
    From Sinai's smoking top,
    Sayin', "Moses lead de people,
    Till I shall bid you stop."
    Cho.—Didn't, etc.

61

SWING LOW SWEET CHARIOT

Arranged by J. Rosamond Johnson

To Mrs. Arthur Curtiss James

look'd ov er Jor dan, an' what did I see, Comin' for to car-ry me home, A

you get-a dere be-fo'- I do, Tell

band of an gels com in' af-ter me, Com-in' for to car-ry me home. If

all my friends I'm com-in'- too, O,

Swing low sweet char-i-ot,_ Com-in' for to car-ry me

home, Swing low sweet char-i-ot,_ Com-in' for to car-ry me

Slower and dying away softly

home, Com-in' for to car-ry me home.__ R.H.

Slower and slower dying away softly

UP ON DE MOUNTAIN

Arranged by J. Rosamond Johnson

Way up on de moun-tain, Lord! ___ Moun - tain
One day Lord, ___ one day Lord, ___ Walk - in'

top, ___ Lord! I heard God talk - in' Lord!
'long ___ Lord, Wid hung down head ___ Lord!

Chil - lun, ___ de char - iot stop ___ Lord!
Chil - lun, ___ an ach - in' heart ___ Lord!

70

LIT'LE DAVID PLAY ON YO' HARP

Arranged by J. Rosamond Johnson

To David Mannes

quit 'till his work was done.___ Jos-hua was de son of Nun___ He nev-er would

quit 'till his work was done.___ Lit'-le Dav-id play on yo' harp, Hal-le - lu, hal - le-

lu, Lit'-le Dav-id play on yo' harp, hal - le - lu.___ Lit'-le Dav-id play on yo' harp, Hal-le -

lu, hal - le - lu, Lit'-le Dav-id play on yo' harp, hal-le-lu_____ ja.___

DIE IN DE FIEL'

Arranged by J. Rosamond Johnson

To Mrs. Francis C. Barlow

what a you say, broth-ers, A - bout dat Gos-pel war, An' I

will die ____ in de fiel', will die ____ in de fiel',

will die ____ in de fiel' I'm on my jour-ney

home Sing it ov-ah I   home. ____

69

RIDE ON, MOSES

Arranged by J. Rosamond Johnson

ALL GOD'S CHILLUN GOT WINGS

Arranged by J. Rosamond Johnson

To Otto H. Kuhn

3. I got a harp, you got a harp, All o' God's Chil-lun got a harp, When I get to heab'n I'm goin' to take up my harp, I'm goin' to play all ov - ah God's Heab'n, ____ Heab'n, ____ Heab'n, ____ Ev-y-bo-dy talk-in' 'bout heab'n ain't goin' dere, Heab'n ____ Heab'n ____ I'm goin' to play all ov - ah God's Heab'n. ____

I got shoes, you got shoes, All o' God's Chil-lun got

shoes   When I get to heab'n I'm goin' to put on my shoes, I'm goin' to

walk all ov ah God's Heab'n, ___ Heab'n, ___ Heab'n, ___ Ev-'y bo dy talk in' 'bout

heab'n aint goin' dere, Heab'n, ___ Heab'n ___ I'm goin' to walk all ov ah God's

Heab'n ___ I'm goin' to walk all ov ah God's Heab'n, ___ I'm goin' to walk all ov ah God's Heab ___

'n, I'm goin' to walk all ov ah, goin' to talk all ov ah God's Heab ___ 'n.

a tempo   *rall.*   *rit.*   *slower*

DERE'S NO HIDIN' PLACE DOWN DERE

Arranged by Lawrence Brown

To Carl Van Vechten

GIMME DAT OL'-TIME RELIGION

Arranged by J. Rosamond Johnson

To Joel E. Spingarn

LIS'EN TO DE LAM'S

Arranged by J. Rosamond Johnson

To Mary Frances Nail

79

HE'S JUS' DE SAME TODAY

Arranged by J. Rosamond Johnson

80

Mo - ses' time is jus _ de same _ to - day. Is _
Dan - iels' time is jus _ de same _ to - day.

RESPONSE

jus _____ de same to - day, _ Jus' _____ de same to - day, _ An' de

molto ritard.

God dat _ lived in Mo - ses' time is jus' de same _ to - day.
Dan - iels'

molto ritard.

Repeat for Verses D.S. 𝄋 | Last time

When day. _____

D.S. 𝄋

81

STAN' STILL JORDAN

Arranged by J. Rosamond Johnson

To My Mother, Helen Louise Johnson

Slowly (*With steady rhythm*)

Stan' still __ Jor - dan, Stan' still Jor - dan, Stan' still Jor - dan, Lord I can't stan' __ still.

I got a moth-er in heav - en, I got a moth-er in heav - en,
When I get up __ in glo - ry, When I get up __ in glo - ry,

I got a moth-er in heav - en, Lord, I can't stan' __ still.
When I get up __ in glo - ry, Lord, I can't stan' __ still.

Stan' still — Jor - dan, Stan' still Jor - - - dan.

Stan' still, Jor - dan, Lord, I can't stan' — still.

Jor - - dan riv - - er, Jor — dan riv - - er,

Jor - - dan riv - er, is chil - ly and cold. —

84

SOMEBODY'S KNOCKIN' AT YO' DO'

Arranged by *J. Rosamond Johnson*

To Samuel Coleridge-Taylor

SINGIN' WID A SWORD IN MA HAN'

Arranged by J. Rosamond Johnson

To Azalia Hackley

(Melody by courtesy of Miss H. B. Lee, Palmer Memorial Institute, Sedalia, N. C.)

Sing-in' wid a sword in ma han'. Pur-ti-est sing-in' ev-er I heard, 'Way ov-ah on de
Pur-ti-est shout-in' ev-er I saw, 'Way ov-ah on de

hill, De an-gels sing an' I sing too, Sing-in' wid a sword in ma han', Lord,
hill, De an-gels shout an' I shout too, Shout-in' wid a sword in ma han', Lord,

Sing-in' wid a sword in ma han', in ma han', Lord, Sing-in' wid a sword in ma
Shout-in' wid a sword in ma nan', in ma han', Lord, Shout-in' wid a sword in ma

han'. Sing-in' wid a sword in ma han', _ Lord, Sing-in' wid a sword in ma
han'. Shout-in' wid a sword in ma han', _ Lord, Shout-in' wid a sword in ma

EXTRA VERSES

Purtiest preachin' ever I heard,
Way ovah on de hill,
De Angels preach an' I preach'd too,
Preachin' wid a sword in ma han', Lord,
Preachin' wid a sword in ma han', Lord,
Preachin' wid a sword in ma han'.

Purtiest prayin' ever I heard,
Way ovah on de hill,
De Angels pray an' I pray'd too,
Prayin' wid a sword in ma han', Lord,
Prayin' wid a sword in ma han', Lord.
Prayin' wid a sword in ma han'.

Purtiest mournin' ever I heard,
Way ovah on de hill,
De Angels mourn an' I mourn'd too,
Mournin' wid a sword in ma han', Lord,
Mournin' wid a sword in ma han', Lord,
Mournin' wid a sword in ma han'.

I COULDN'T HEAR NOBODY PRAY

Arranged by J. Rosamond Johnson

To W. E. Burghardt DuBois

MY WAY'S CLOUDY

Arranged by J. Rosamond Johnson

Sen' dem an - gels down, Dere's fire a - mong dem Me - tho - dis'__ Oh,
Sen' dem an - gels down, He missed de soul he thought he had,__ Oh,

sen' - a dem an - gels down Old __
sen' - a dem an - gels down. O, breth er - en,

My __ way, __ my way's clou - dy, my __ way, Go

sen' - a dem an - gels down, O, breth er - en down __

IT'S ME, O, LORD

Arranged by J. Rosamond Johnson

To Natalie Curtis Burlin

94

95

I GOT A HOME IN-A DAT ROCK

Arranged by Lawrence Brown

To Walter and Gladys White

see? Poor man Laz-rus, poor as I, When he died he foun' a home on high. He had a

home in-a dat Rock, Don't you see? Rich man, Di-ves, He lived so well, Don't you

see? Rich man, Di-ves, He lived so well, Don't you see? Rich man,

rit.   *a tempo*

Di-ves, he lived so well, when he died he foun' a home in Hell, He had no

home in-a dat Rock, Don't you see? God gave Noah de Rain-bow sign, Don't you

see? God gave Noah de Rain-bow sign, Don't you see? God gave Noah de Rain-bow sign, No mo

rit.

wa-ter but fire nex' time, Bet-ter get a home in-a dat Rock, Don't you see?

BY AN' BY

Arranged by J. Rosamond Johnson

To Mrs. William Curtis Demorest

Lively

O, by an' by,—

by an' by — I'm gwinter lay down my heavy load.— O,

DEEP RIVER

Arranged by J. Rosamond Johnson

To Booker T. Washington

100

WHO DAT A-COMIN' OVAH YONDAH?

Arranged by J. Rosamond Johnson

ROLL JORDAN, ROLL

Arranged by J. Rosamond Johnson

To Paul Robeson

hear ol' Jor-dan roll. Sing it ov-ah, Oh, roll. O,

Roll Jor-dan, roll, Roll Jor-dan,

roll, I want-er go to heav-'n when I die,— To

hear ol' Jor-dan roll.

DE BLIN' MAN STOOD ON DE ROAD AN' CRIED

Arranged by J. Rosamond Johnson

To Sidney Woodward

what kind o' shoes am dose you wear,_____ Cry-in'
dese shoes I wear am de Gos-pel shoes,_____

what kind o' shoes am dose you wear,_____ Cry-in'
dese shoes I wear am de Gos-pel shoes,_____

O,_____ my Lord, Save-a me De blin' man

stood on de road an' cried. Cry-in' cried._____

repeat for verses   *last time*

109

ROLL DE OL' CHARIOT ALONG

Arranged by J. Rosamond Johnson

To Elbridge L. Adams

Lively

Roll de ol' cha-riot a-long, yes, roll de ol' cha-riot a-long, yes, Roll de ol' cha-riot a-long Ef yo don't hang on be-hin'. O Christ-ans, Roll de ol' Cha-riot a-long, yes, roll de ol' cha-riot a-long, yes, roll de ol' cha-riot a-long, Ef yo' don't hang on be-hin': Ef yo

CALVARY

Arranged by J. Rosamond Johnson

To my Father, James Johnson

Response

Cal - va - ry,_____ Cal - va - ry,— Cal - va -

f

ry,_____ Cal - va - ry,— Cal - va - ry,

Cal - va - ry,_____ Sho'___ly He died on

Repeat for Verses   *D.S.* 𝄋 *Last time*

Cal - - va - ry.·   ry._____

𝄋 *D.S.*   *R.H. ritard.*

113

STEAL AWAY TO JESUS

Arranged by J. Rosamond Johnson

To Roland Hayes

Je - sus! Steal a-way, steal a-way home, ___ I ain't got long to stay here. My Lord, He calls me, He calls me by the thun-der, The trum-pet sounds with-in-a my soul, I ain't got long to stay here.

GWINE UP

Arranged by J. Rosamond Johnson

To Percy Grainger

See de hea-ben-ly lan';— Gwine to see my robe an' try it on,
See de hea-ben-ly lan';— Dem-a snow white an-gels I shall see,

See de hea-ben-ly lan',— It am bright-er dan-a dat glit-ter-in' sun,
See de hea-ben-ly lan',— Den de deb - bil am-a gwine to let - a me be,

See de hea-ben-ly lan'! Oh, yes, I'm Gwine up, gwine up,
See de hea-ben-ly lan'! Oh, yes, I'm

gwine all de way, Lord, Gwine up gwine up to

1.
D.C. to 𝄋   Last time
see de hea-ben-ly lan'!—   see de hea-ben-ly lan'!
D.C. to 𝄋

119

I'M TROUBLED IN MIND

Arranged by J. Rosamond Johnson

To Marian Anderson

O, GAMBLER, GIT UP OFF O' YO' KNEES

Arranged by J. Rosamond Johnson

MY LORD'S A-WRITIN' ALL DE TIME

Arranged by J. Rosamond Johnson

To Louis Graveure

Chorus

sees all you do, He hears all you say,— My Lord's a-writ-in' all de time. Oh, He

sees all you do, He hears all you say,— My Lord's a-writ-in' all de time. Oh, He time. When

LEAD

RESPONSE

I was down in— E - gypt's lan'— My Lord's a-writ-in' all de

Christ-ians, you had— bet - ter pray,— My Lord's a-writ-in' all de

time, I heard some talk of de prom - ised lan',—

time, For Sa - tan's round you— 'ev' - ry day,—

124

My Lord's a-writ-in' all de time. Oh,
My Lord's a-writ-in' all de _____ time. Oh, He

Chorus

sees all you do, He hears all you say, __ My Lord's a-writ-in' all de

time Oh, He sees all you do, He hears all you say, __

My Lord's a-writ-in' all de time yes, all de time.

GIT ON BOARD, LITTLE CHILLEN

Arranged by Lawrence Brown

To Laura J. Heathfield

GWINTER SING ALL ALONG DE WAY

Arranged by J. Rosamond Johnson

pen-tance an' sal - va-tion, Am grav-en dere in gold We'll
Christ an' all his ar-my, On dat ce-les-tial _____ shore. Oh, I'm a gwin-ter

sing, _____ gwin-ter sing, _____ gwin-ter sing all a - long de

way, Oh, I'm a gwin-ter sing, _____ gwin-ter sing, _____ gwin-ter

sing all a - long de way _____ all a - long de way.

WHO'LL BE A WITNESS FOR MY LORD?

Arranged by J. Rosamond Johnson

To Carl Van Vechten

clean as yo' han', An' his strength be-came de same as an-y natch'-al man. O,

Response

Sam-son was a wit-ness for my Lord, O, Sam-son was a wit-ness for my Lord, O,

Sam-son was a wit-ness for my Lord, O, Sam-son was a wit-ness for my Lord. Now

Lead

Dan-iel was a He-brew child, He went to pray to his God a-while, De

king at once for Dan-iel did sen', An' he put him right down in de lion-'s den;

God sent His ang-els de lion-s for to keep, An' Dan-iel laid down an' went to sleep. Now

Response (Lively)

Dan-iel was a wit-ness for my Lord, Now Dan-iel was a wit-ness for my Lord.

Dan-iel was a wit-ness for my Lord, Dan-iel was a wit-ness for my Lord. O,

who'll be a wit-ness for my Lord? O, who'll be a wit-ness for my Lord? My

soul is a wit-ness for my Lord, My soul is a wit-ness for my Lord.

KEEP A-INCHIN' ALONG

Arranged by J. Rosamond Johnson

To John W. Work

died one time gwine-ter die no mo' Mas-sa Je-sus is com-in' bye an' bye. O, I
you in de Lord and de Lord in you, Mas-sa Je-sus is com-in' bye an' bye. O
can I die when I'm in de Lord? Mas-sa Je-sus is com-in' bye an' bye. How

died one time gwine-ter die no mo' Mas-sa Je-sus is com-in' bye an' bye.
you in de Lord and de Lord in you, Mas-sa Je-sus is com-in' bye an' bye. Keep a-
can I die when I'm in de Lord? Mas-sa Je-sus is com-in' bye an' bye.

in-chin' a-long, Keep a- in-chin' a-long, Massa Je-sus is com-in' bye an' bye. Keep a-

Repeat for Verses | *last time*

in-chin' a-long like a po' inch worm, Mas-sa Je-sus is com-in' bye an' bye. O, bye.
How

WHERE SHALL I BE WHEN DE FIRS' TRUMPET SOUN'?

Arranged by J. Rosamond Johnson

March Tempo
Where shall I be when de firs' trum-pet _ soun'
Gwine to try on ma robe when de firs' trum-pet _ soun'
ff
mf
Where shall I be, When it soun' so_ loud, When it soun' so loud till it
Gwine to try on ma robe,
ff
Repeat for Verses
Last time
wake up de dead;— Where shall I be when it soun'. O, Breth - er - en soun'
(or) O, Sis - ter - en
mf
mp

PETER, GO RING DEM BELLS

Arranged by J. Rosamond Johnson

To "Singing" Johnson

Moderately Lively

Oh, Pe-ter, go ring dem bells, Pe-ter, go ring dem bells,

Pe-ter, go ring dem bells, I heard f'om heav'n to-day. Oh, day. I

Won-der where my mother is gone, I won-der where my moth-er is gone, I
Won-der where sis-ter Ma-ry is gone, I won-der where sis-ter Ma-ry is gone, I

won-der where my moth-er is gone I heard f'om heav'n to-day. I
won-der where sis-ter Ma-ry is gone I heard f'om heav'n to-day. I

137

NOBODY KNOWS DE TROUBLE I SEE

Arranged by J. Rosamond Johnson

To Henry E. Krehbiel

(Note: This is a rare version.)

141

EV'RY TIME I FEEL DE SPIRIT

Arranged by J. Rosamond Johnson

To Walter F. White

1 Repeat pp Omit after last verse
2
fire an smoke. (2) An' all a- O, Ev'-ry
all was mine.
but not de- soul.
sfz
f
time I feel de spir-it, move-in' in my heart, I will
pray. O, ev'-ry time I feel de spir-it, move-in' in my
ff
1 Omit after last verse
2 Last time
heart, I will pray (3) Jor-dan pray.
D.S.

FATHER ABRAHAM

Arranged by J. Rosamond Johnson

To Daisy Tapley

144

I'M A-ROLLIN'

Arranged by J. Rosamond Johnson

To Robert Edmond Jones

DIDN'T MY LORD DELIVER DANIEL?

Arranged by J. Rosamond Johnson

To Robert Russa Moton

He - brew chill - un fom de fi - er - y fur - nace, An' why not ev - e - ry man. Did - n't my Lord de - liv - er Dan - iel __ de - liv - er Dan - iel __ de - liv - er Dan - iel, __ Did-n't my Lord de - liv - er Dan iel __ An' why not a ev - e - ry man. De

149

moon run down in a pur-ple stream, De sun for— bear to— shine, An'
win' blows eas' an' de win' blows wes', It blows like de judg-a-ment day, An'

ev - e - ry star— dis - ap - pear, King — Je - sus— shall-a be
ev-'ry 'po' soul dat nev-er did pray'll, be glad— to pray dat

mine, De day. Did-n't my Lord de-liv-er Dan - iel de-liv-er Dan - iel de-liv-er

Dan -iel, Did-n't my Lord de-liv-er Dan-iel — An' why not-a ev-e-ry man. I

150

Set my foot on de Gos-pel ship, an' de ship be - gin to _ sail, It

land-ed me o-ver on Can-aan's shore An' I'll nev-er come back no _ mo'. Did-n't

my Lord de-liv-er Dan-iel,_ de-liv-er Dan-iel,_ de-liv-er Dan - iel,_ Did-n't

my Lord de-liv-er Dan - iel _____ An' why not - a ev-e-ry man.

O, WASN'T DAT A WIDE RIVER?

Arranged by J. Rosamond Johnson

river of Jor - dan is so wide, One mo' riv - er to cross. I
Sat - an am noth - in' but a snake in de grass, One mo' riv - er to cross. If

mf

don't know how to get on de oth - er side; One mo' riv - er to
you ain't might - y care - ful he will hol' you fas', One mo' riv - er to

1
2

cross. Ol' cross. O, was - n't dat a wide riv - er, dat riv - er of Jor - dan, Lord,

Wide____ riv - er! Dere's one mo' riv - er to cross.____

KEEP ME F'OM SINKIN' DOWN

Arranged by J. Rosamond Johnson

Oh,_____ Lord,_____ Oh,_____ my Lord! Oh,_____ my good Lord! Keep me f'om sink-in' down._____ Oh,_____ Lord,_____ Oh,_____ my Lord! Oh,_____ my good Lord! Keep me f'om sink-in' down. I

tell you what I mean to do; Keep me f'om sink-in' down: I
look up yon-dah an' what do I see; Keep me f'om sink-in' down: I

mean to go to hea-v'n too, Keep me f'om sink-in' down I
see de an-gels beck-on-in' me, Keep me f'om sink-in' down.

Oh,___ Lord,___ Oh,___ my Lord! Oh,___ my good Lord!

Keep me f'om sink-in' down ___ f'om sink-in' down.

DE BAND O' GIDEON

Arranged by J. Rosamond Johnson

To Mary White Ovington

JOHN SAW THE HOLY NUMBER

Arranged by J. Rosamond Johnson

John saw, Oh, John saw, John saw the ho-ly num-ber
sit-ting on the gol-den al-tar___ al-tar.___
Worth y, worth-y is the Lamb, is the Lamb, is the Lamb, Oh,
Ma-ry wept, an' Mar-tha cried, Mar-tha cried, Mar-tha cried, Oh,

Worth - y   worth - y   is   the   Lamb,   Sit - ting   on   the   gold - en
Weep - ing   Ma - ry   weeps   no   more,   Sit - ting   on   the   gold - en

al - tar,   Oh,   al - tar   John   saw,   Oh,   John   saw,

John   saw   the   ho - ly   num - ber   sit - ting   on   the   gold - en

al - tar   al - tar   On   the   gold - en   al - tar

GIVE ME JESUS

Arranged by J. Rosamond Johnson

Moderately Slow *(with Religious Devotion)*

Oh, __ when I come to die, __ Oh, __
Dark __ mid-night was my cry, __ Dark __

when I come to die, Oh, __ when I come to die, Give me
mid-night was my cry, Dark __ mid-night was my cry, Give me

Je - sus. In dat morn-in' when I rise, __ Dat morn-in' when I
Je - sus I __ heard a mourn-er say, __ I heard a mourn-er

MY LORD, WHAT A MORNIN'

Arranged by J. Rosamond Johnson

To Mary E. Floyd

(The title of this song has at times been erroneously printed "My Lord, What A Mourning")

162

hear de trum - pet sound,
hear de sin - ner moan, To wake de na-tions un-der ground,
hear de Christ - ians shout,

Look-in' to my God's right hand, When de stars be-gin to fall. My Lord, what a

morn-in', My Lord, what a morn-in', My Lord, what a morn-in', When de

stars be-gin to fall, When de stars be-gin to fall.

Repeat for Verses | *Last time*

② You'll
③ You'll

163

O, ROCKS DON'T FALL ON ME

Arranged by J. Rosamond Johnson

To Fritz Kreisler

look o - vah yon-dah on Je-ri-cho's walls, Rocks _ an' moun - tains don't fall on me, An'
ey - ah - ry star re - fus - es to shine Rocks _ an' moun - tains don't fall on me, I
see dem sin-ners trem-ble an' fall, _ Rocks _ an' moun-tains don't fall on me. O,
know dat King Je-sus will - a be mine, _ Rocks _ an' moun-tains don't fall on me. De
in - a dat great great judg-a-ment day, Rocks _ an' moun-tains don't fall on me, De
trum-pet shall soun' An' de dead shall rise, Rocks _ an' moun-tains don't fall on me, An'
sin-ners will run to de rocks an say _ Rocks _ an' moun-tains don't fall on me.
go to de man-sions in-a de skies, _ Rocks _ an' moun-tains don't fall on me.
ff
pp
mf
f

166

DONE FOUN' MY LOS' SHEEP

Arranged by J. Rosamond Johnson

To H. T. Burleigh

That jes lef' Him nine-ty-nine, Go to de wild-er-ness, seek an' fin', Ef you fin' him, bring him back, Cross de shoul-ders, Cross yo' back; Tell de neigh-bors all a-roun', Dat los'sheep has done be foun! Done foun'my los' sheep,— Done foun'my los' sheep,— Done foun'my los' sheep. In dat Res - sur - rec-tion Day

sin-ner can't fin no hid-in' place, Go to de moun-tain, de moun-tain move;

Run to de hill, de hill run too. Sin-ner man trab-lin' on tremb-ling groun', Po' los' sheep aint

neb-ber been foun' Sin-ner why don't yo' stop and pray, Den you'd hear de Shep-herd say, Done

foun' my los' sheep, Done foun' my los' sheep, Done foun' my los' sheep.

WHAT YO' GWINE TO DO WHEN YO' LAMP BURN DOWN?

Arranged by J. Rosamond Johnson

Slowly with meditation

O,— po' sin-ner, O,— now is yo' time,— O— po' sin-ner, O,— What yo' gwine to do when yo' lamp burn down

Fin' de Eas', fin' de Wes', What yo' gwine to do when yo' lamp burn down.
Head got wet wid de mid-night dew, What yo' gwine to do when yo' lamp burn down.

Fire gwine to burn down de wil-der-ness, What yo' gwine to do when yo' lamp burn down.
Morn-in'— star was a wit-ness too, What yo' gwine to do when yo' lamp burn down.

O,— po' sin-ner, O,— now is yo' time,— O,— po' sin-ner, O,—

What yo' gwine to do when yo' lamp burn down. *Fine*

Dey whipp'd Him up an dey whipp'd Him down,
Dey nail'd His han' an dey nail'd His feet,

What yo' gwine to do when yo' lamp burn down. Dey whipp'd dat man all
What yo' gwine to do when yo' lamp burn down. De ham-mer was heard on Je-

o - vah town, What yo' gwine to do when yo' lamp burn down.
rus - a - lem street, What yo' gwine to do when yo' lamp burn down.

D.S. %
D.S. %

HALLELUJAH!

Arranged by J. Rosamond Johnson

172

been to de sea an' I've done been tried, ___ Been down ___ in - to the sea; O, I've
Christ-ians, ___ Can't you ___ rise an' tell, ___ Been down ___ in - to the sea; The ___
you don't ___ b'lieve I've ___ been re - deemed, Been down ___ in - to the sea; Just
born of ___ God, I ___ know I am, Been down ___ in - to the sea; I'm

repeat verses ad lib.

been to de sea an' I've been bap-tize', ___ Been down ___ in - to the sea. O,
glo - ries ___ of Im - man-u - el? ___ Been down ___ in - to the sea. If, ___
watch my ___ face for the gos-pel gleam, ___ Been down ___ in - to the sea. I'm
pur-chased by the ___ dy - ing Lamb, Been down ___ in _____ - to the sea.

Hal - le - lu - jah an' a hal - le ___ lu - jah ___

Hal-le - lu - jah, Lord ___ I've been down ___ in - to the sea. -to the sea.

173

CRUCIFIXION

Arranged by J. Rosamond Johnson

To Roland Hayes

174

tree, an' He nev-er said a mum-ba-lin' word. Not a word, not a word, not a word. They

pierced him in the side, an' He nev-er said a mum-ba-lin' word, They pierced him in the

side, an' He nev-er said a mum-ba-lin' word. Not a word, not a word, not a word.____ The

blood came twink-lin' down, an' He nev-er said a mum-ba-lin' word; The blood came twink-lin'

175

down,   an' He nev - er said a mum-ba-lin' word.   Not a word,   not a

gradually growing softer and slower

word, not a word. ———   He bow'd his head an' died,   an' He

pp   *f tempo*

pp

nev-er said a mum-ba-lin'   word,   He bow'd his head an'   died,   an' He

nev-er said a mum-ba-lin'   word;   Not a   word, not a   word, not a   word. ——

gradually slower and softly dying away

r.h.   *r.h.*   *r.h.*

l.h.   *l.h.*   *ppp*

176

UNTIL I REACH-A MA HOME

Arranged by J. Rosamond Johnson

some say gim - me sil - vah, an' some say gim - me gol', But

I say gim - me Je - sus mos' pre - cious to ma soul. Dey

say dat· John de Bap - tis' was noth - in' but a Jew, But de

ho - ly Bi - ble tells us, Dat he was a preach - er too. O, broth-ers,
O, sis - ters, Un-

til I reach - a ma home,_____ Un-

til I reach - a ma home._____ I

nev-ah in-ten' to give de jour-ney ov-ah, un-

til I reach ma home._____

I DONE DONE WHAT YA' TOL' ME TO DO

Arranged by J. Rosamond Johnson

To Clarence B. Ashenden

done-a what ya' tol' me to do. So glad __ I done done, So glad __ I done done So __
(After last verse only) Thank God __ I done done, Thank God __ I done done Thank

Ending for all verses. | *Last ending*

glad I done done, I done done a-what ya' tol' me to do. Tol' me to done a-what ya' tol' me to do.
God I done done,

YOU MAY BURY ME IN DE EAS'

Arranged by Lawrence Brown

To Alec Rowley

Lento

You may bur-y me in de Eas', You may

bur-y me in de Wes', But I'll hear de trump-et soun' __ in dat morn-in', In dat

morn - in', my Lord, How I long_to go, For to hear de trump-et soun',_ In dat

morn - in'. Good ole Christ-ians in dat day, Dey'll take wings an' fly a-way, For to

hear de trump-et soun'__ in dat morn - in', In dat morn - in', my Lord,

How I long_ to go, For to hear de trump-et soun',_ In dat morn - in'

YOU GOT A RIGHT

Arranged by J. Rosamond Johnson

You got a right, I got a right, We all got a right, to the tree of life. Yes, tree of life. De ve-ry time I thought I was los' De dun-geon shuck an' de chain fell off. You may hinder me here But you can-not dere, 'Cause

God in de heav'n gwin-ter ans - wer prayer (O bre-ther-en)
(O sis-ter - en)

You got a right, I got a right, We all got a right to de tree of life Yes, tree of life.

WEARY TRAVELER

Arranged by J. Rosamond Johnson

To John McCormack

Slowly *(with steady swing)*

Let us

Cheer the wea - ry trav - el - er; Let us cheer the wea - ry trav - el - er, A - long the heav - en - ly way.

187

THE SECOND BOOK OF
NEGRO SPIRITUALS

THE SECOND BOOK OF
NEGRO SPIRITUALS

Edited with an introduction by
JAMES WELDON JOHNSON

Musical arrangements by
J. ROSAMOND JOHNSON

CONTENTS

CONTENTS

THE SECOND BOOK OF
NEGRO SPIRITUALS

PREFACE

In this the second Book of American Negro Spirituals we are continuing the work of putting these songs, characteristically arranged, in permanent form.

The present volume contains most of those old favorites that largely for reasons of space were left out of the first. In it will be found the familiar version of *Nobody Knows De Trouble I See*. (The first volume contained the rare version of this song.) There will also be found the stirring and triumphant *Walk Together Children*, the apocalyptic *'Zekiel Saw De Wheel*, and the poignantly sad *Sometimes I Feel Like a Motherless Child*. Other old favorites are: *Sinner Please Don't Let Dis Harves' Pass, Gwineter Ride Up In De Chariot, Lord I Want To Be A Christian In-a My Heart, Gimme Yo' Han', I Know De Lord's Laid His Hands On Me, Walk In Jerusalem Jus' Like John, De Ol' Ark's A-Moverin'*, and *Humble Yo'self De Bell Done Ring*. Moreover, we are confident that even those who are familiar with the Spirituals will be astonished at the number of songs, lesser known but of remarkable beauty and quality, here included. These are some of the songs in this volume which need only to be heard to be loved: *My Soul's Been Anchored In De Lord, God's A-Gwineter Trouble De Water, Dere's A Han'writin' On De Wall, Walk, Mary, Down De Lane, Mary Had A Baby, Chilly Water, I Want God's Heab'n To Be Mine, Death's Gwineter Lay His Cold Icy Hands On Me, I Want to Die Easy When I Die, My Lord Says He's Gwineter Rain Down Fire, Same Train, In Dat Great Gittin' Up Mornin'*.

It would almost seem that the number of beautiful Spirituals is inexhaustible. In these two volumes of The Book of American Negro Spirituals there have been collected and arranged six score songs, and, despite the number of lost Spirituals, there are many score more. And the Spirituals, in a limited degree, are still in the making; as is evi-

11

PREFACE

denced by the recent splendid collection made at the Penn Normal, Industrial and Agricultural School, St. Helena Island, South Carolina, by N. G. J. Ballanta, an accomplished African musician. Considering the common source of the Spirituals, the absence of monotony is more than surprising. Those who have heard J. Rosamond Johnson and Taylor Gordon or Paul Robeson and Lawrence Brown in recital must have remarked the unexpected variety displayed in a program made up exclusively of Spirituals. These artists generally sing at a concert twenty to twenty-five numbers, and yet they avoid approaching anything like sameness. They often conclude programs even of such length with the audience clamoring for more.

What is the secret of the wide variety and perennially fresh appeal of the Spirituals? How is it that an audience can listen to them for two hours without interlude and without boredom or satiety? The Negro took as his basic material just his native African rhythms and the King James version of the Bible and out of them created the Spirituals;[1] how then was he able to produce a body of five or six hundred religious songs with so little monotony of treatment and effect? One explanation is the fact that although the Spirituals in a general classification fall under the heading "religious songs," all of them are by no means religious in a narrow or special sense. All of them are by no means songs of worship, though having a religious origin and usage. In the Spirituals the Negro did express his religious hopes and fears, his faith and his doubts. In them he also expressed his theological and ethical views, and sounded his exhortations and warnings. Songs of this character constitute the bulk of the Spirituals. But in a large proportion of the songs the Negro passed over the strict limits of religion and covered nearly the whole range of group experiences—the notable omission being sex. In many of the Spirituals the Negro gave wide play to his imagination; in them he told his stories and drew his morals therefrom; he dreamed his dreams and declared his visions; he uttered his despair and prophesied his victories; he also spoke the group wisdom and expressed the group philosophy of life. Indeed, the Spirituals taken as a whole contain a record and a revelation of the deeper thoughts and experiences of the Negro in this country for a

[1] For an account of the origin and development of the Spirituals see preface to first Book of American Negro Spirituals (New York, 1925), pp. 19–23.

12

PREFACE

period beginning three hundred years ago and covering two and a half centuries. If you wish to know what they are you will find them written more plainly in these songs than in any pages of history. The Spirituals together with the secular songs—the work songs and the sex songs—furnish a full expression of the life and thought of the otherwise inarticulate masses of the Negro race in the United States.

A further explanation of the variety of the Spirituals lies in the Negro's many-mooded nature; his sensitiveness and quick response to the whole gamut of human emotions. And what a range he has! I do not believe there is any other people in the world that can be so lugubriously sad as the Negro, or so genuinely gay. An added explanation is found in his lively imagination, not yet wholly dulled by stereotyped ideas. For illustration: the age-old symbol of death's convoy is a boat crossing a stream or a ship leaving one port and entering another. The Negro has made frequent use in the Spirituals of this classic symbol; but turn to the song, *Same Train*, and you will see that he does not hesitate to scrap the stereotype and create a new symbol out of his own everyday experiences. He dares to do this, and, what is more important, he does it to the point of perfection. The imagery is not lessened; and see how the inevitability of death is insistently suggested in the inevitably recurring "Same train. Same train."

Above all, the Negro was using as his medium the infinitely varied rhythmic patterns of his native African music, to which he had added a new-found harmonic strength and melodic beauty.[2] For these reasons he was able to fashion many kinds of songs from what was practically the same materials. Songs that are the cry of a lost soul and songs that are the voice of an army with banners. Songs that are crooning lullabies and songs like the thunders about Sinai. Pass from the pathos of *Sometimes I Feel Like A Motherless Child* to the thrill of *Walk Together Children*, from the intenseness of *Stan' Still Jordan* to the exultancy of *Joshua Fit De Battle Ob Jericho*, from the lull of *Swing Low Sweet Chariot* to the trumpet-tongued proclamation of *Go Down Moses*, and you will get an idea of the wide musical and poetical range spanned by the Spirituals that I have been trying to indicate.

[2] For a discussion of African rhythms and the "swing" of the Spirituals see *ibid.*, pp. 17–18 and 28–30. See also foreword to St. Helena Spirituals, N. G. J. Ballanta, New York, 1925.

PREFACE

The present volume contains sixty-one numbers. Every kind of Spiritual, as in the first Book, is here represented. There is, indeed, one kind that is extremely rare, the Spiritual based on the birth or infancy of Jesus. The crucifixion and the resurrection have been treated over and over by the creators of the Spirituals, but apparently the birth of Christ made very little appeal to them, and there are practically no "Christmas Spirituals." This is to me a quite curious fact. It would seem that the lowly birth of Jesus, from which more than one analogy could have been drawn, would have furnished the makers of the Spirituals with an inspiring theme, but, for reasons I am not able to give, it did not. It may be that the old-time plantation preacher, nonplussed by the Immaculate Conception, touched upon the birth of Christ only lightly or not at all, and, therefore, that part of the story of his life was not deeply impressed upon the bards.[3] Or it may be that the Negro preferred to think of Jesus as God, as almighty, all-powerful to help; and this idea of him could not easily be reconciled with his being born of a woman. Jesus, in the older Spirituals, is generally given a title of power. Sometimes he is referred to as "Massa Jesus"; most often he is called "King Jesus." One of the noblest and most inspiriting of all the Spirituals runs:[4]

> Ride on Jesus, Ride on Jesus.
> Ride on Conquering King;
> I wanter go to heab'n in de mornin'.

The reason may be due in part to the fact that the anniversary of the birth of Christ was not, in the South, in any sense a sacred or religious holiday. Up to within recent years, at least, it has been celebrated chiefly with gunpowder and whiskey. It has there been the most secular, even the most profane of all holidays. In slavery times it was the one day on which the slaves were given a sort of freedom. The liberty of coming and going was greatly enlarged. On many plantations whiskey was distributed. The day was one given over to a good time; to singing, dancing and visiting; to guzzling, gluttony and

[3] For reference to the work and offices of these bards see preface to first Book of Spirituals, pp. 21–23.
[4] For discussion of the poetry of the Spirituals see *ibid.*, pp. 38–42.

14

PREFACE

debauchery. It is possible that it was a conscious part of the scheme of slavery to make Christmas a day on which the slaves through sheer excess of sensuous pleasure would forget their bonds. One sure result was that there was destroyed in the minds of the slaves any idea of connection between the birth of Christ and his life and death. At any rate, there are at most only two or three "Christmas Spirituals," and occasional lines referring to the birth of Jesus Christ here and there in other songs. In 1919 Miss Natalie Curtis published two songs, one she had found in Virginia entitled *Dar's A Star In De East,* and the other a song she got from St. Helena Island, South Carolina, entitled *Mary Had A Baby.* There are several versions of this latter song in the Ballanta collection. There was included in the Hampton collection (1909) a song entitled, *Rise Up Shepherd An' Foller.* Both *Mary Had A Baby* and *Rise Up Shepherd An' Foller,* characteristically harmonized and arranged, are in this volume.

In my opinion, the above observations are fairly good evidence that the "Christmas Spirituals" and the other songs containing lines referring to Christ's birth are of recent date. It is more than probable that they belong to a period quite some time after Emancipation; to a period in which there had come the development of a new idea not only of Christmas, but of Christ. This conclusion is further borne out by my inability through racking my early memories to recall anything like a "Christmas Spiritual," and by the fact that no Spiritual of that sort is found in the early standard collections.

There is no way of telling how much of this music has been lost beyond hope of retrieval. For more than a century the Negro had been singing his Spirituals before their beauty and significance were in the slightest degree recognized. It is only within the past fifty or sixty years that any worth-while effort has been made to collect and record these songs; and it is not probable that the original collections were anything near exhaustive. But the Negro and the world are lucky in that so great a mass of them has been saved. I say lucky because it was largely a matter of chance that practically all of this music was not completely lost. The Negro has been doubly lucky, because his music was preserved by others when he himself was unable to do the work, and because his amanuenses, in addition to their other qualifica-

15

PREFACE

tions, were men and women of honesty. The Spirituals were first collected and set down by white people from the North who came in contact with the Negroes of the South during or immediately after the Civil War.[5] These collectors might have omitted to make the exclusive Negro origin of the songs a part of the record; and so the task might have devolved some day upon the Negro to establish his title as their sole creator. The Negro was likewise lucky with regard to his folk tales. The plantation stories were collected and set down by a Southern white man,[6] who, had he failed to tell specifically where he got the tales and about their creators, might in time have been passed as an original and imaginative writer *influenced* by Negro life.

The Negro has not had such good fortune with the other folk contributions he has made to the common store of American art. Dancing, so far as it is a native art in America, has been dominated almost absolutely by Negro influence; and yet the Negro has received only the scantiest credit for his contribution. Of course, professional exponents who draw upon or exploit Negro dances do not pause to explain the fact, nor could they reasonably be expected to do so. I know of but one exception, Mr. Vernon Castle, perhaps the most noted, and, by the way, an Englishman, who always danced to the music of a colored band, and never failed to state that most of his dances had long been done ''by your colored people,'' as he put it. Moreover, in great measure, the credit has been deliberately taken away; as witnessed by the number of white vaudeville performers and dancing instructors who promptly advertised themselves as ''originators'' of the world-encircling ''Charleston.'' Something of the same sort has happened with regard to Negro secular music. The early black-face minstrels simply took such Negro songs as they wished and used them. The first of the so-called Ragtime songs to be published were actually Negro secular folk songs that were set down by white men, who affixed their own names as the composers. In fact, before the Negro succeeded fully in establishing his title as creator of his secular music the form was taken away from him and made national instead of racial. It has been developed into the distinct musical idiom by which America expresses it-

[5] For a history of the collection and preservation of the Spirituals see *ibid.*, pp. 46–49.

[6] The plantation stories were collected and published by Joel Chandler Harris under the title of *Uncle Remus*.

16

self popularly, and by which it is known universally. For a long while the vocal form was almost absolutely divorced from the Negro; the separation being brought about largely through the elimination of dialect from the texts of the songs. The vogue of the Blues, and the record of the origin and development of this latest vocal form written down by W. C. Handy and Abbe Niles, have gone far to recover the ground lost in this field. There was at one time much publicity discussion as to which of the white Jazz band leaders was entitled to the credit of originating the instrumental form. Now, however, there is a widening acknowledgment of the fact that this form, which has reached a point of development where it is commanding the attention of scholarly musicians, is based upon Negro rhythms and polyphonic structure, and was used by colored bands as far back as twenty years ago. By way of further digression, it is interesting to speculate upon how far one of the most distinctive qualities of Jazz, the orchestral tone-color, is to be credited to the Negro in a negative sense, indeed, to a lack. The charm of this tone-color results from the unorthodox composition of the Jazz orchestra. The composition of the Jazz orchestra is based upon instruments that do not demand long and arduous and expensive training under a master, but which, for anybody with a natural musical ear, are easily self-taught. The violin, which is the mainstay of the orthodox orchestra, is in the Jazz orchestra entirely eliminated or reduced to a place of least importance. The instrumental combination which gives to good Jazz music its peculiar power of excitation to motor response was not consciously designed; it, like Topsy, just happened and grew. At the same time, it cannot be overlooked that the two instruments which play the greater part in producing this effect are the African drum and the Aframerican banjo.

There are no indications that the high regard attained by the Spirituals will be followed by any marked decline in interest. The vogue of these songs is by no means a suddenly popular fad; it has been reached through long and steady development in the recognition of their worth. Three generations ago their beauty struck a few collectors who were attuned to perceive it. A little while later the Fisk Jubilee Singers made them known to the world and gave them their first popularity, but it was a popularity founded mainly on sentiment. The chief effect of this slave music upon its white hearers then was that they were touched and moved with deepest sympathy for the "poor Negro." The Spirituals passed next through a period of investigation and study and of artistic appreciation. Composers began afterwards to arrange them so that their use was extended to singers and music-lovers. And then they made their appearance on concert programs and their appeal was greatly broadened. Today, the Spirituals have a new vogue, but they produce a reaction far different from the sort produced by their first popularity; the effect now produced upon white hearers is not sympathy for the "poor Negro" but admiration for the creative genius of the race. The Spirituals have passed through and withstood many untoward conditions on the long march to the present appreciation of their value; they have come from benighted disregard through scorn, apathy, misappraisal, even the ashamedness and neglect of the race that created them, to where they are recognized as the finest distinctive artistic contribution America can offer the world. The history of the Spirituals is sufficient evidence that they possess the germ of immortality. It is far this side of prophecy to say that they will last as long as anything artistic that has thus far been produced on this continent.

Has this music in any way been a vital force? Has its power brought about any change? What modification has it worked upon the nation and within the Negro? The Spirituals have exerted a gentle and little-considered influence for a good many years. For more than a half century they have touched and stirred the hearts of people and effected a softening down of some of the hard edges of prejudice against the Negro. Measured by length of years, they have wrought more in sociology than in art. Indeed, within the past decade and especially within the past two or three years they have been, perhaps, the main force in breaking down the immemorial stereotype that the Negro in America is nothing more than a beggar at the gate of the nation, waiting to be thrown the crumbs of civilization; that he is here only to receive; to be shaped into something new and unquestionably better. The common idea has been that the Negro, intellectually and morally empty, is here to be filled, filled with education, filled with religion, filled with morality, filled with culture, in a word, to be made into what is considered a civilized human being. All of this is, in a measure, true; but in a larger measure it is true that the Negro is the possessor of a wealth of natural endowments; that he has long been a generous giver to America; that he has helped to shape and mold it; that he has put an indelible imprint upon it; that America is the exact America it is today because of his influence. A startling truth it is that America would not be precisely the America it is except for the silent power the Negro has exerted upon it, both positive and negative. I say the truth is startling because I believe the conscience of the nation would be shocked by contemplation of the effects of the negative power the Negro has involuntarily and unwittingly wielded. This awakening to the truth that the Negro is an active and important force in American life; that he is a creator as well as a creature; that he has given as well as received; that he is the potential giver of larger and richer contributions, is, I think, due more to the present realization of the beauty and value of the Spirituals than to any other one cause.

The Spirituals have only just begun to exert an appreciable influence in art; and, strange to say, not at all or very little have they affected the field of music. The recent emergence of a younger group of Negro artists, preponderantly literary, zealous to be racial, or to put it better, determined to be true to themselves, to look for their art material within rather than without, got its first impulse, I believe, from the new evaluation of the Spirituals reached by the Negro himself. Almost suddenly the realization broke upon the Negro that in the Spirituals the race had produced one of the finest examples of folk-art in the world. The result was a leaping pride, coupled with a consciousness of innate racial talents and powers, that gave rise to a new school of Negro artists. In fact, it gave rise to what can be termed The Negro Youth Movement, a movement which embodies self-sufficiency, self-confidence and self-expression, and which is lacking in the old group sensitiveness to the approbation or opinion of its white environment. Of course, there have before been individual Negro writers actuated in the same way as this younger school, who have drawn deeply on racial resources and material, but this group motivation, operating upon a larger group which is aware and responsive, is a new and significant thing.

The Negro was a long time in coming to a realization of the true worth of the Spirituals [7]—and there are still some faultily educated colored people who are ashamed of them—but when he did, his eyes were opened to all of his own cultural resources.

Before going into how much farther the Spirituals may advance as a force in art, let us, in passing, give a moment's consideration to the distance the younger school of Negro artists may cover. It is a fact beyond question that the Negro in the United States has produced fine and distinctive folk-art. Aframerican folk-art, an art by Africa out of America, Negro creative genius working under the spur and backlash of American conditions, is unlike anything else in America and not the same as anything else in the world; nor could it have been possible in any other place or in any other times. With the close of the creative period of the Blues, which appears to be at hand, it is probable that the whole folk creative effort of the Negro in the United States will have come to an end. The Blues, in their primitive form, are pure folk songs. They are the philosophical expression of the individual contemplating his situation in relation to the conditions surrounding him. In this respect they are the opposite of the Spirituals, which are an expression of the group. And, as follows naturally, the Spirituals are essentially group songs, while the Blues are essentially solos. The date of the origin of the Blues cannot be exactly fixed, but the internal evidence of the songs indicates that it is comparatively recent. The philosophical comment in them is upon conditions which Negroes in the South have had to face only since the Civil War: the courts, the law, the savagery of officers of the law, the chain gang, the life of work on the railroads, and life in the cities; in a word, the Blues contain the judgments of the ignorant and lower Negro masses upon all the hard conditions of modern life they have been called on to meet. Another evidence of this more or less recent origin is a new note in them that is foreign to the traditional traits; there is a note of pessimism, even of cynicism. Mr. Abbe Niles in his foreword to "Blues" declares this philosophy is that of choosing as the reaction to disaster laughter instead of tears, and says it is summed up in the line:

Got de blues, and too dam' mean to cry.

[7] For an account of the attitude of the colored people toward the Spirituals see preface to first Book of Spirituals, pp. 49–50.

PREFACE

But this philosophizing, no matter upon what subject, generally centers around the separation of the man from the woman or the woman from the man by the intervening conditions; and so for the most part, these songs resolve themselves into the lament of a lover who is feeling "blue." Many of the lines contain flashes of real primitive poetry. For these reasons, the Blues are even more interesting and valuable as poetry than they are as music.[8] For example, the lines:

> My man's got teeth like a lighthouse by de sea,
> An' when he smiles he th'ows a light on me.

The production of folk-art requires a certain naïveté, a certain insouciance, a sort of intellectual and spiritual isolation on the part of the producing group that makes it indifferent to preconceived standards. All of these, the Negro in the United States is fast losing, and inevitably. The bulk of this Aframerican folk production has been music, music of many kinds, songs of many kinds; but the urge and necessity upon the Negro to make his own music, his own songs, are being destroyed not only by the changing psychology but by such modern mechanisms as the phonograph and the radio. In fact, there are phonograph companies that make a business of furnishing colored people with close imitations of Negro folk songs. The production of genuine Aframerican folk-art must, sooner or later, cease. In time, even Negro dialect will be only a philological curiosity. Now, can the individual Negro artist produce a conscious art that will be as distinctively Aframerican as is the folk-art?

I doubt the possibility for the individual artists, especially the preponderating literary group, to produce anything comparable to the folk-art in distinctive values. Common education, common interests, a common language—all the environmental forces are against it. Through sheer conscious effort and determination something "different" might be produced, but most likely it would be something artificial and stillborn. I do not believe such effort is worth the while. But I do believe these artists can and will bring something new and vital *into American art.* They will bring to it something from the store of

---

[8] For a more detailed discussion see foreword to *Blues*, A. & C. Boni, New York, 1926, and the valuable treatise on Negro work songs and the Blues, *Negro Workaday Songs*, Odum and Johnson, University of North Carolina Press, 1926

PREFACE

their racial genius:—warmth, color, movement, rhythm, abandon, freshness of unfettered imagination, the beauty of sensuousness, the depth and swiftness of emotion. This they can do by drawing fully on their racial resources and material, and through not being afraid of the truth. The writers, especially, have large opportunity to do their share by portraying Negro life as they alone can see and understand and interpret it, by painting it in true colors from the depths to the heights. And what a range they have! From the drollest comedy, through romance to the most overwhelming tragedy. No other group encompasses in its actual history and experiences in this country so wide and varied an emotional sweep as the Negro; and none but Negro artists can ever give it fullest artistic play. I am not even suggesting racial limits for Negro artists; any such bounds imposed would be strangling. I am rather re-stating what is axiomatic; that the artist produces his best when working at his best with the materials he knows best.

The environmental forces operating upon the individual Negro artists will not, I think, apply so inflexibly to those who may come in the fields of painting and the plastic arts. And less inflexibly still will they apply to the musicians. And this brings us back to a brief consideration of the Spirituals as a force in music. What is to be the future of this music? Will it continue only as folk songs, to become some day merely an exhibit in our museum of artistic antiquities, or is it to be a force in the musical art of America? It is safe to say that for many generations the Spirituals will be kept alive as folk songs. I think it equally safe to say they will some day be a strong element in American music. They possess the qualities and powers; the trouble, so far, has been their almost absolute neglect and rejection by our serious composers. Our lesser musicians have been wiser and more diligent; they have taken the music the Negro created in lighter moods —Ragtime, Jazz, Blues—and developed it into American popular music. Indeed all the major folk creations of the Negro have been taken up and developed, except the Spirituals. The secular music has been developed and has become national and international; the dances have been developed with an almost equal result; we see even the development or degeneration of "Uncle Remus" into the popular bed-time stories. Why cannot this nobler music of the Negro in the hands of

22

PREFACE

our serious composers be wrought into the greater American music that has so long been looked for?

I do not think the composers of any country have at their hands an unexplored mine of richer materials than American composers have in the Spirituals. Do our composers want themes for development into the greater forms, themes rooted in our artistic subsoil and having the vital spark of life? Let us suggest a few from the Spirituals; a choice can be made almost at random, sweet, plaintive, rhythmic, majestic:

Swing Low Sweet Chariot

Sinner Please Don't Let Dis Harves' Pass

My Lord Says He's Gwineter Rain Down Fire

PREFACE
Go Down Moses

I do not believe American composers will always overlook and pass over this fund of source material.

In the arrangements in this volume Mr. J. Rosamond Johnson has observed the same fidelity to the true characteristics of this music as he did in the First Book. However, he has here striven for greater simplicity. These arrangements will, we believe, prove interesting to the musician, but they will not be found too difficult for the average pianist.

JAMES WELDON JOHNSON

Great Barrington, Massachusetts.
1926.

DE OL' ARK'S A-MOVERIN' AN' I'M GOIN' HOME

To Mr. and Mrs. Lawrence Langner

See dat sis - ter all dressed so fine? She
See dat broth - er all dressed so gay? O,
See dat sis - ter dere com - in' so slow? She
'Tain't but one - a thing on - a my min'. My

Verses ad lib

ain't got Je - sus on - a her min'.
death's gwineter come for to car - ry him a - way.
wants to go to heab'n 'fore de heab'n door close.
sis - ter's gone to heab'n an' - a lef' a me be - hin'. O, de

ol' ark's a - mov - er - in', a - mov - er - in', a - mov - er - in', De

ol' ark's a - mov - er - in', An' I'm goin' home. O, de   I'm goin' home. O, de

ol' ark she reel, De ol' ark she rock, D'ol' ark she land-ed on de moun-tain top. O, de

moun-tain top. O, de   ol' ark's a - mov - er - in', a - mov - er - in', a - mov - er - in'. De

ol' ark's a - mov - er - in', An' I'm goin' home. O, de   I'm goin' home.

MY LORD SAYS HE'S GWINETER RAIN DOWN FIRE

To Mr. Melville Charlton

29

SOMETIMES I FEEL LIKE A MOTHERLESS CHILD

To Miss Ruth Hale

home; _____ A long ways__ from home. True

-believ - er, A long ways__ from home, _____ A

long ways__ from home. Some-times I feel like I'm

al - mos' gone, Some-times I feel like I'm al - mos' gone,

31

Some-times I feel like I'm al - mos' gone; Way up in de heab'n - ly lan',_____ Way up in de heab'n - ly lan'. True_ be - liev - er, way up in de heab'n - ly lan',_____ way up in de heab'n - ly

32

lan'. Some-times I feel like a moth-er-less child,

Some-times I feel like a moth-er-less child,

Some-times I feel like a moth-er-less child, A

long ways from home.

33

NOBODY KNOWS DE TROUBLE I SEE

(Familiar Version)

To Mr. Harold K. Guinzburg

34

tho' you see me goin' 'long so, Oh, yes, Lord: I

have my tri - als here be - low, ___ Oh, yes, Lord. Oh!

No-bod-y knows de troub-le I see, No-bod-y knows but Jes-us; ___

No-bod-y knows de troub-le I see, Glo - ry, hal-le-lu - jah!

slower

slower

36

MY SOUL'S BEEN ANCHORED IN DE LORD

To Mr. Nathaniel Dett

Moderately Slow (*with steady swing*)

In de Lord, in de Lord, — My soul's been an - chored in de Lord; In de Lord, in de Lord, — My soul's been an-chored in de Lord. In de Lord. Be-

IN DAT GREAT GITTIN' UP MORNIN'

To Mr. George Gershwin

I'm-a goin' to tell you 'bout de com-in' of de Sav-iour, Fare you well, Fare you well. Fare you well, Fare you well.

Dere's a bet-ter day a-com-in', Fare you well, Fare you well; Oh, preach-er,
Pray-er mak-er, pray no mo'— Fare you well, Fare you well; For de las'
Dat de time shall be no long-er, Fare you well, Fare you well; For judg-ment
Den you hear de sin-ner say-in' Fare you well, Fare you well; Down I'm roll-in'

fol' yo' bi-ble, Fare you well, Fare you well.
soul's con-ver-ted, Fare you well, Fare you well.
day is com-in', Fare you well, Fare you well.
down I'm roll-in', Fare you well, Fare you well.

In dat great git-tin' up morn-in'—

Fare you well, Fare you well; In dat great git-tin' up morn-in' Fare you well, Fare you well.

De — Lord — spoke to Ga-briel, Fare you well, Fare you well; Go - look be-
Lord how loud — shall I blow it, Fare you well, Fare you well; Blow it right
Ga — briel — blow yo' trum pet, Fare you well, Fare you well; Lord, how loud
Place one foot up — on de dry lan' Fare you well, Fare you well; Place de oth - er
Hell shall be un — cappd an' burn-in' Fare you well, Fare you well; Den de drag-on

hin' de al - tar, Fare you well, Fare you well. Take — down de sil - vah trum-pet,
calm an' ea - sy, Fare you well, Fare you well. Do — not — a - larm my peo-ple,
shall I blow it, Fare you well, Fare you well. Loud as sev-en — peals of thun-der,
on de sea, — Fare you well, Fare you well. Den you'll see de — cof-fins bust-in',
shall be loos-end, Fare you well, Fare you well. Where you run-nin' po' sin - ner,

Fare you well, Fare you well. Blow yo' trum - pet Ga - briel; Fare you well,
Fare you well, Fare you well. Tell 'em to — come to judg - ment; Fare you well,
Fare you well, Fare you well. Wake de liv — in' — na - tions, Fare you well,
Fare you well, Fare you well. See de dry bones — come a-creep - in', Fare you well,
Fare you well, Fare you well. Where you run-nin' po' sin - ner, Fare you well,

41

Fare you well.   In dat great git-tin' up morn-in'— Fare you well, Fare you well;
Fare you well.
Fare you well.
Fare you well.
Fare you well.

In dat great git-tin' up morn-in', Fare you well, Fare you well.   Den you'll see po'
See de moon
See de ele-
Den you'll cry out for
Say-in' A-men to

sin-ners ris-in' Fare you well, Fare you well; Den you'll see de worl' on fiah,
a — bleed-in' Fare you well, Fare you well; See de stars— a — fall-in'
ments a-melt-in' Fare you well, Fare you well; See de — forked— light-nin'
cold — wat-er, Fare you well, Fare you well; While de Chris-tians shout in glor-y,
yo' dam-na-tion, Fare you well, Fare you well; No mer-cy — for po' sin-ner,

Fare you well, Fare you well: In dat great git-tin' up morn-in', Fare you well,
Fare you well, Fare you well:
Fare you well, Fare you well:
Fare you well, Fare you well:
Fare you well, Fare you well:

Fare you well; In dat great git-tin' up morn-in' Fare you well, Fare you well.

Hear de rum-blin' of de thun-der, Fare you well, Fare you well. Earth shall reel
Den you'll see de Chris-tian ris - in' Fare you well, Fare you well. Den you'll see de
See dem march-in' home to hea-b'n, Fare you well, Fare you well. Den you'll see my
Wid — all His ho - ly an-gels, Fare you well, Fare you well. Take de right-eous
Dere dey live wid God for-ev - er, Fare you well, Fare you well. On de right hand

an' — tot - ter, Fare you well, Fare you well. In dat great git-tin' up morn-in'—
right - eous march-in' Fare you well, Fare you well.
Je - sus com - in', Fare you well, Fare you well.
home to glor - y, Fare you well, Fare you well.
side of my Sav-i-our, Fare you well, Fare you well.

Fare you well, Fare you well; In dat great git-tin' up morn-in' Fare you well, Fare you well.

YOU GO, I'LL GO WID YOU

To the memory of George Walker

You go, I'll __ go wid you; O-pen yo' mouth, I'll __ speak for you:

Lord, if I go, tell me what to say, Dey won't be-lieve in me. Oh, me. Now

Lord, I give my - self to Thee, 'Tis all dat I can do; If thou should draw thy-

self from me,— Oh, with-er shall I flee? De arch-an-gels done droop dere wings,

Went up on Zi-on's hill to sing; Climb-in' Ja-cob's lad-der high, Gwine

reach heab'n by an' by. Oh, you go, I'll— go wid you; O-pen yo' mouth, I'll—

— speak for you; Lord, if I go, tell me what to say, Dey won't be-lieve in me. Oh, me.

I WANT TO DIE EASY WHEN I DIE

To Mr. F. E. Miller

Moderately Slow = *(with steady swing)*

I want to die

eas - y, when I die,___ when I die;___ I want to die

eas - y, when I die,___ when I die;___ I want to die

eas-y, when I die,___ Shout sal - va-tion as I fly,___ I want to die

46

48

eas - y, when I die, ___ when I die; __

I want to die eas - y, when I die, __ Shout sal -

va - tion as I fly; __ I want to die eas -

y, when I die, when I die. __

49

SINNER, PLEASE DON'T LET DIS HARVES' PASS

To Mr. Will C. Handy

please, don't let dis har-ves' pass, dis har-ves' pass. Sin-ner,

please, don't let dis har-ves' pass, har-ves' pass ___ Sin-ner,

please, don't ___ let dis har-ves' pass, An' die, an'

Little Slower

lose ___ yo' soul at las' ___ yo' soul at las'. ___

52

RELIGION IS A FORTUNE I REALLY DO BELIEVE

To Mr. Clement Wood

Moderately Lively

Oh, re-

lig - ion is a for - tune, I real - ly do be - lieve, Oh, re-
sit down in de king-dom, I real - ly do be - lieve, Gwine-ter

lig - ion is a for - tune, I real - ly do be - lieve, Oh, re-
sit down in de king-dom, I real - ly do be - lieve, Gwine-ter

lig - ion is a for-tune, I real - ly do be - lieve, Where
walk a - bout in Zi - on, I real - ly do be - lieve, Where

53

Sab - baths have no end. ___ Gwineter ___
Sab - baths have no ___ end. ___

Where you been po' mourn-er, where you been so long; Bow low down in de
Where you been po' sin-ner, where you been so long; Bow low down in de

val-ley for to pray, An' I ain't done pray-in' yet. O, yet. Gwineter
val-ley for to pray, An' I ain't done pray-in' yet. ___ Gwineter

See my Sis-ter Ma-ry I real-ly do be-lieve, Gwineter see my Sis-ter
Walk-a wid de An-gels I real-ly do be-lieve, Gwineter walk-a wid de

Ma-ry, I real-ly do be-lieve, Gwineter see ol' Brud-der Jon-ah, I
An-gels I real-ly do be-lieve, Gwineter see my Mas-sa Je-sus, I

real-ly do be-lieve, Where Sab-baths have no end.___ Gwineter
real-ly do be-lieve, Where Sab-baths have no end.___

Where you been po' mourn-er, where you been so long; Bow low down in de
Where you been po' sin-ner, where you been so long; Bow low down in de

val-ley for to pray, An' I aint done pray-in' yet. yet.___
val-ley for to pray, An' I aint done pray-in' yet. yet.___

55

GREAT DAY

To Mr. Andrea de Segurola

Great — day!

Great day, de right-eous march-in', Great — day! God's gwine-ter build up Zi - on's walls. Zi - on's walls. De

char - iot rode on de moun-tain top, —
is de day of — ju - bi-lee,
take my breas'-plate, sword in han' —
want no cow - ards in our ban', —

Great day!

WALK IN JERUSALEM JUS' LIKE JOHN

To Mr. Franklin P. Adams

I want— to be read-y,

I want— to be read-y,— I want— to be read-y,— to

walk in Je-ru-sa-lem jus' like John. jus' like John. John said— de cit-y was
John! Oh, John! what
Pet-er was preach-in' at

SAME TRAIN

To Mr. Carl Van Vechten

60

WHEN I FALL ON MY KNEES

(WID MY FACE TO DE RISIN' SUN)

To the memory of Bob Cole

break bread to - ged - der, on our knees, yes, on our
drink wine to - ged - der, on our knees, yes, on our

knees; Let us break bread to - ged - der, on our
knees; Let us drink wine to - ged - der, on our

knees, yes, on our knees; When I fall on my
knees, yes, on our knees; Wid my

knees, Wid my face to de ris - in' sun; Oh, Lord, have

mer - cy on me. _____ Let us me. _____ Let us

praise God to-ged-der, on our knees, on our knees, Let us

praise God to-ged-der, on our knees, on our knees; When I

fall on my knees, wid my face to de ris-in' sun, Oh,

Lord, have mer-cy on me.

RISE UP SHEPHERD AN' FOLLER

To Mr. Julius Bledsoe

DO DON'T TOUCH-A MY GARMENT, GOOD LORD, I'M GWINE HOME

To Miss Florence Mills

Moderately Lively

Do don't touch - a my gar - ment,— Good Lord, Good Lord.

Do don't touch - a my gar - ment,— Good Lord, I'm gwine home.— Oh,

Lord, I'm gwine home.— To yo'. God— an' my God,— Good

Lord, Good Lord. To yo' God _ an' my God, _ Good

Lord, I'm gwine home. _ To

Lord I'm gwine home. _

Do don't touch - a my slip - pers, _ Good Lord, Good Lord.

Do don't touch - a my slip - pers, _ Good Lord, I'm gwine home. _ Oh,

touch me not ___ lit - tle Ma - ry, ___ Good Lord, Good Lord.

Touch me not lit-tle Ma - ry, ___ Good Lord, I'm gwine home. ___ (Oh breth-er-en)

Do don't touch-a my star-ry crown, Good Lord, Good Lord.

Do don't touch-a my star-ry crown, Good Lord, I'm gwine home. ___ To

LORD, I WANT TO BE A CHRISTIAN IN-A MY HEART

To Mr. Clarence Cammeron White

want to be like Ju-das in-a my heart._____ In-a my
want to be like Je-sus in-a my heart._____

heart _____ In-a my heart,_____ Lord, I

Last time

ff — mp *mp Last time*

little slower

want to be a Chris-tian in-a my heart,_____ In-a my

little slower *mp*

[1]

[2] *omit after last verse* [3] *last time*

heart._____ Lord I heart._____

pp

73

A LITTLE TALK WID JESUS MAKES IT RIGHT

To my sister A. M. Edwards

broth--er, I re--mem--ber, when I was a sin--ner lost, I
cried "Have mer--cy Je--sus," But still my soul was toss'd; 'Til I
heard King Je--sus say, "Come here, I am de way;" An' a
lit--tle talk wid Je--sus, makes it right._____ Some-

lit - tle talk wid Je - sus, makes it right, all right.

Lit - tle talk wid Je - sus, makes it right, all right. Lord,

trou - bles of ev - 'ry kind, Thank God, I'll · al - ways find, Dat a

lit - tle talk wid Je - sus, makes it right.____

PO' MOURNER'S GOT A HOME AT LAS'

To Mr. Harry T. Burleigh

Slowly (*prayerfully*)

Hm_____ Hm_____ my Lord!_____ Hm_____ Po'

mourn-er's got a home at las'. Mourn-er's got a home at las'. O,

Mourn - er,__ mourn - er,__ Ain't you tired o' mourn-in',__
Sin - ner,__ sin - ner,__ Ain't you tired o' sin - nin',__

Bow down on-a yo' knees an'___ join de ban' wid de an - gels. O,

No harm,___ Lord, no harm, Go tell brud-der E - li - jah,___

No harm,___ Lord, no harm, Po' mourn-er's got a home at las'___ Dere's

mourn-er's got a home at las'. O, gamb-ler,___ gamb-ler,___

79

Ain't you tired o' gamb-lin'___ Bow down on-a yo' knees an'___ join de ban' wid de an-gels.___ Hm___ Hm___ my Lord,___ Hm___ Po' mourn-er's got a home at las!___

ritard. e dim.

80

MARY AN' MARTHA JES' GONE 'LONG
(TO RING DEM CHARMIN' BELLS)

Note—"Charmin" is the dialect equivalent of "chiming"

To Mrs. Edith Barbee Moseley

Free grace an' dy - in' love, To ring dem charm-in' bells. Cry-in' bells. O, de

preach-er an' eld - er jes' gone 'long, Preach-er an' eld - er jes' gone 'long,
moth-er an' fath - er jes' gone 'long, Moth-er an' fath - er jes' gone 'long,

Preach-er an' eld - er, jes' gone 'long—To ring dem charm-in' bells. Yes. My ol'
Moth-er an' fath - er, jes' gone 'long—To ring dem charm-in'

bells. Cry-in' Free grace an' dy - in' love, Free grace an' dy - in' love,

82

GOD'S A-GWINETER TROUBLE DE WATER

To my brother "Jim"

Moderately Slow *(with reverence)*

Wade ____ in de' wa-ter, chil-dren, Wade ____ in de wa-ter,chil-dren,

Wade ____ in de wa-ter, chil-dren, God's a-gwine-ter trou-ble de wa-ter.

See dat host all dressed in white,— God's a-gwine-ter trou-ble de wa-ter; De

See dat ban' all dressed in red,— God's a-gwine-ter trou-ble de wa-ter; Looks

lead-er looks like de Is-rael-ite,— God's a-gwine-ter trou-ble de wa-ter.

like—de ban' dat Mos-es lead, God's a-gwine-ter trou-ble de wa-ter.

Wade— in de wa-ter, chil-dren, Wade— in de wa-ter, chil-dren, Wade in de

wa-ter, chil-dren, God's a-gwine-ter trou-ble de wa-ter. wa-ter.—

GIMME YO' HAN'

To Mr. Richard Copley

Very Lively (*with jubilant spirit*)

O,

gim-me yo' han', Gim-me yo' han'— All I want is de love o' God;— Gim-me yo' han',

gim-me yo' han', You mus' be lov-in' at God's com-man'. O, God's com-man'. You

say you're aim-in' for de skies,— You mus' be lov-in' at God's com-man' Why
say de Lord has set you free,— You mus' be lov-in' at God's com-man' Why
seek God's grace but don't seek right;— You mus' be lov-in' at God's com-man' Dey

don't you-quit yo' tell-in' lies,—You mus' be lov-in' at God's com-man'. You —
don't you- let yo' neigh-bor be,—You mus' be lov-in' at God's com-man'. Some —
pray in de day, but none at night,—You mus' be lov-in' at God's com-man', O,

gim-me yo' han'— gim-me yo' han'— All I want is de love o' God;—

Gim-me yo' han'— gim-me yo' han'— Yeu mus' be lov-in' at God's com-man', Yes, you

mus' be lov-in' at God's com-man'.

87

I WANT GOD'S HEAB'N TO BE MINE

Melody collected by Harry Block

To Miss Fania Marinoff

want God's hea-b'n to be mine, To be mine, to be mine; Yes, I

want God's hea-b'n to be mine, Save me, Lord, save me. Yes, I me. I

hail   to   my moth-er,   my   moth-er_   hail   to   me_   an' de
hail   to   my lead-er,   my   lead-er_   hail   to   me_   an' de

las' word I heard her   say,   Save me, Lord, save   me. I   me. Yes, I
las' word I heard him   say,

want God's 'hea-b'n to   be mine,   to   be mine,   to   be mine; Yes, I

want God's hea-b'n to   be mine,   Save me, Lord, save me. Yes, I   me.

89

I HEARD DE PREACHIN' OF DE WORD O' GOD

To Mr. Paul Robeson

heard   de preachin'of de El-der,   Preachin'de word,   preachin' de word, I

heard   de preachin'of de El-der,   Preachin'de word o'   God. I   God. How

long did it rain? Can an-y one tell? Preachin' de word o' God, For

for - ty days an' nights it fell, Preachin' de word o' God. How

long was Jon-ah in de bel-ly of de whale? Preachin' de word o' God, 'Twas

three whole days an' nights he sailed, Preachin' de word o' God. When

I was a mourner I mourned 'til I got through, Preachin' de word o' God. My

knees got ac-quainted wid de hill-side too, Preachin' de word o' God. I

heard de preachin' of de El-der, Preachin' de word, preachin' de word; I heard de

Little slower

preachin' of de El-der, Preachin' de word o' God. Yes, preachin' de word o' God.

DEATH'S GWINETER LAY HIS COLD ICY HANDS ON ME
(*Familiar Version*)

To Miss Rita Romilly

Slowly (*with pathos*)

Death____ is gwine-ter lay his cold i-cy hands on me, Lord, on me____ Death____ is gwine-ter lay his cold i - cy hands on me. ____ O, me. ____ One

morn-in' I was walk-in' 'long, I heard a voice an'-

saw no man; Said go in peace an' sin no mo', Yo'

sins fo'-giv'n an' yo' soul set free. One o' dese morn-in's it

won't be long, You'll look fo' me, an' I'll be gone, Yes,

DEATH'S GWINETER LAY HIS COLD ICY HANDS ON ME
(*Rare Version*)

To Mme. Marguerite d'Alvarez

O, sin-ner, sin-ner, you bet-ter pray, Death's gwine-ter lay his cold i - cy hands on me, Or yo' soul will get los' at de judg-ment day, Death's gwine-ter lay his cold i - cy hands on me.

97

98

YOU MUS' HAB DAT TRUE RELIGION

To Miss Rebecca West

Whar you gwine po' sin - nah,
Whar you gwine po' li - ar,
Whar you gwine po' gam - bler,
Whar you gwine back slid - er,
Whar you gwine, I say, I'm a

gwine down to de rib-buh ob Jor-dn, You can't cross dere. O, dere. Lord knows, You

Repeat for Verses   *Last time*

Mus' hab dat true re-li-gion, You mus' hab yo' soul con-ver-ted, You

mus' hab dat true re-li-gion, You can't cross dere. O, yes, you dere.

101

TOO LATE
(OR DONE CARRY DE KEY AN' GONE HOME)

To the memory of Mme. C. J. Walker

lock de do', Car-ry de key an' gone home. Lock de do' an' take de key,—

O, Lord! too late; Lock de do' an' take de key,— Car-ry de key an gone home.

Too late,— too late, false pre-ten-der, Hm— too late; Too late, too late, back-sli-der,

Car-ry de key an' gone home. Mas-sa Je-sus lock de do' O,— too late;

Lock de do' an' take de key,_ Car-ry de key an' gone home. Mas-sa Je-sus

lock de do' O, Lord! too late; Lock de do' an' take de key,

Car-ry de key an' gone home. Too late,___ too late, sin-nah, Hm___

too late; Too late,___ too late, sin-nah, Car-ry de key an' gone home.

OH, YES! OH, YES! WAIT 'TIL I GIT ON MY ROBE

To Mr. Alain Locke

come dis night to — sing an' pray, — Oh, yes, Oh, yes, To drive ol' Sat - an
heab-'nly home is — bright an' fair, — Oh, yes, Oh, yes, But migh - ty few can

far a - way, — Oh, yes, Oh, yes. Dat Oh, yes. Oh,
en - ter dere, — Oh. yes,

wait 'til I git on my robe, wait 'til I git on my robe,

Wait 'til I git on my robe, Oh, yes,

Oh, yes. Oh, Oh, yes. Oh,
I went down in de
if you want-er catch dat
what do you think he
bow yo' knees up

val - ley to pray, Oh, yes, Oh, yes. I
heab - 'nly breeze, Oh, yes, Oh, yes. Go
said to me, Oh, yes, Oh, yes. You're too
on de groun', Oh, yes, Oh, yes. An'

106

met ol' Sa - tan — on de way, — Oh, yes,
down in de val - ley on yo' knees an' pray, — Oh, yes,
young to — pray — an' too young to die, — Oh, yes,
ask yo' Lord — to — turn you 'roun' — Oh, yes,

Oh, yes. An' Oh, yes. Oh, wait 'til I git on my robe,
Oh, yes. Now
Oh, yes. Oh,

Wait 'til I git on my robe, Wait 'til I

git on my robe, Oh, yes. Oh, yes. Oh, Oh, yes.

DEATH COME TO MY HOUSE HE DIDN'T STAY LONG

To Mr. James Priaulx

RUN, MARY, RUN
(I KNOW DE UDDER WORL' IS NOT LIKE DIS)

To Miss Marie Cahill

Fire in de Eas' an' fire in de Wes' I
Jor - dan's riv - er is a riv - er to cross, I

know de ud - der worl' is not like dis. Boun' to burn de
know de ud - der worl' is not like dis. Stretch yo' rod an'

wil - der - ness, I know de ud - der worl' is not like dis.
come a - cross, I know de ud - der worl' is

Swing low sweet cha - ri - ot in - to de Eas', I
low sweet cha - ri - ot in - to de Norf, I
not like dis.   if dis was de judg - ment day, I

know de ud-der worl' is not like dis, Let God's chil - dren
know de ud-der worl' is not like dis, Give me de gol' wid -
know de ud-der worl' is not like dis, Ev' - ry sin-ner would

have some peace, I know de ud-der worl' is not like dis, Swing
out de dross, I know de ud-der worl' is not like dis, Swing
want to pray, I know de ud-der worl' is not like dis, Ol'

low sweet cha-ri-ot in - to de Wes' I know de ud-der worl' is
low sweet cha-ri-ot in - to de Sout' I know de ud-der worl' is
trou-ble it come like a gloom-y cloud I know de ud-der worl' is

not like dis. Let God's chil - dren have some res', I
not like dis. Let God's chil - dren sing and shout, I
not like dis. Gad - der thick an' thun - der loud, I

know de ud-der worl' is not like dis. Swing
know de ud-der worl' is not like dis. Now
know de ud-der worl' is _____ not like dis.

Run, Ma - ry, run, Run, Ma - ry, run, Oh,

run, Ma - ry, run, I know de ud - der worl' is

not like dis, Oh, not like dis.

CHILLY WATER

To Mr. Roland Hayes

114

to dat Lam', But I_____ have Je___sus_____ in_a my soul, An' a
to dat Lam', Christ Je____ sus standin' as de cor_ner stone, An' a
to dat Lam', He's watchin' for to bite_ you_ as_a you pass, An' a
to dat Lam', You'd bet-ter be_ ready when de roll_ is call, An' a

Hal - le - lu - jah to dat Lam', O,
Hal - le - lu - jah to dat Lam', Ol'
Hal - le - lu - jah to dat Lam', O,
Hal - le - lu - jah to dat Lam'.

Chil - ly wa - ter, Chil - ly_ wa -

ter, Hal - le - lu - jah to dat Lam'. to dat Lam'.

RISE, MOURNER, RISE

To Mr. Witter Bynner

117

DE ANGEL ROLL DE STONE AWAY

To Mr. William Arms Fisher

soun', De an-gel roll de stone a - way.___ De an-gel way.___ Sis-ter

Ma - ry came a - run - nin',___ at de break o' day,___
look-in' for my Sav-iour,___ tell me where He lay,___
sol-jahs dere a - plen-ty,___ stand-in' by de do',
Pi - late an' his wise men, didn't know what to say,___ De

Brought de news f'om heab-en, De stone done roll a - way. I'm-a
High up on de moun-tain, De stone done roll a - way. De___
But dey could not hin - der, De stone done roll a - way. Ol'___
mir - a - cle was on dem, De stone done roll a - ___ way. De an-gel

roll de stone a - way_____ De an - gel

roll de stone a - way; _____ 'Twas on a bright an shi - ny

morn, When de trum - pet be - gin to soun; De an - gel roll de

stone a - way._____ De an - gel way._____

pp

120

GWINETER RIDE UP IN DE CHARIOT SOON-A IN DE MORNIN'

To Mr. Countée Cullen

mer-cy on me, O, Lord, have mer-cy on me, O, Lord, have_

mer-cy on. me, An' I hope I'll jine de ban! ban! Gwineter

Meet my broth-er dere, yes, soon-a in de morn-in'
Chat-ter wid de an-gels, soon-a in de morn-in'
Meet my Mas-sa Je-sus, soon-a in de morn-in'
Walk and talk wid Je-sus, soon-a in de morn-in'

Meet my broth-er dere, yes, soon-a in de morn-in' Meet my broth-er dere, yes,
Chat-ter wid de an-gels, soon-a in de morn-in' Chat-ter wid de an-gels,
Meet my Mas-sa Je-sus, soon-a in de morn-in' Meet my Mas-sa Je-sus,
Walk and talk wid Je-sus, soon-a in de morn-in' Walk and talk wid Je-sus,

122

soon-a in de morn-in' An' I hope I'll jine de ban'. Gwineter____
soon-a in de morn-in' An' I hope I'll jine de ban'. Gwineter____
soon-a in de morn-in' An' I hope I'll jine de ban'. Gwineter____
soon-a in de morn-in' An' I hope I'll jine de ban'.

O, Lord, have___ mer-cy on me, O, Lord, have

mer-cy on me, O, Lord, have___ mer-cy on me' An' I

hope I'll jine de ban'. ban'. I hope I'll jine de ban'.

Little Slower

MARY HAD A BABY, YES, LORD

To Mr. Walter F. White

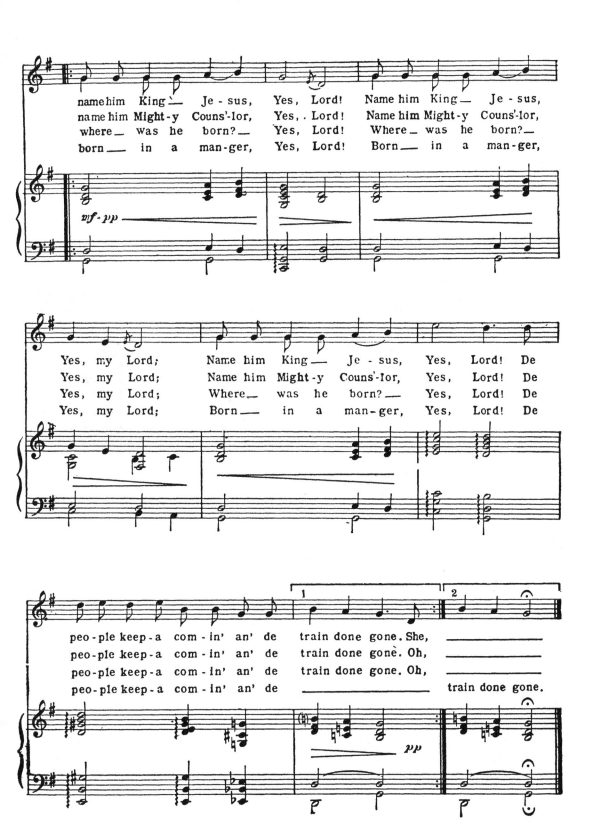

name him King— Je - sus, Yes, Lord! Name him King— Je - sus,
name him Might-y Couns'-lor, Yes, . Lord! Name him Might-y Couns'-lor,
where— was he born? Yes, Lord! Where— was he born?—
born— in a man-ger, Yes, Lord! Born— in a man-ger,

Yes, my Lord; Name him King— Je - sus, Yes, Lord! De
Yes, my Lord; Name him Might-y Couns'-lor, Yes, Lord! De
Yes, my Lord; Where— was he born?— Yes, Lord! De
Yes, my Lord; Born— in a man-ger, Yes, Lord! De

peo-ple keep-a com - in' an' de train done gone. She,
peo-ple keep-a com - in' an' de train done gone. Oh,
peo-ple keep-a com - in' an' de train done gone. Oh,
peo-ple keep-a com - in' an' de train done gone.

I'M GWINE UP TO HEAB'N ANYHOW

To my sister Grace Nail Johnson

DE ANGELS IN HEAB'N GWINETER WRITE MY NAME

To Mr. Edward Wassermann

Moderately Fast

O, write my name,— O, write my name;

O, write my name,— De Angels in de hea-b'n gwineter write my name.

write my name. Write my name when-a you get home,— De
Write my name in de Book of life,— De

Angels in de hea-b'n gwineter write my name. Yes, write my name wid-a
Angels in de hea-b'n gwineter write my name. Yes, write my name in de

gold-en pen,_ De Angels in de heab'n gwineter write my name.
drip-pin' blood,_ De Angels in de heab'n gwineter write my name.

O, write my name,_ O, write my name;

O, write my name,_ De Angels in de heab'n gwineter write my name.

ALL I DO, DE CHURCH KEEP A-GRUMBLIN'

To Mr. and Mrs. Alfred A. Knopf

130

Try my bes' for to serve my Master, Try my bes' for to
Try my bes' for to fol-ler my Lead-er, Try my bes' for to
Kneel an' pray, so de dev-il won't harm me, Try my bes' for to
I'm gwine cling to de ship o' Zi-on. Try my bes' for to

serve my Lord; Try my bes' for to serve my Mas-ter,
serve my Lord; Try my bes' for to fol-ler my Lead-er,
serve my Lord; Kneel an pray so de dev-il won't harm me,
serve my Lord; I'm gwine cling to de ship o' Zi-on,

1.
Hal-le-lu - - jah.
Hal-le-lu - - jah.
Hal-le-lu - - jah.

2
Hal-le-lu - - jah.

All I

131

do, de church keep a grumb-lin' All I

do, Lord, all I do._____ All I do, de church keep a

grumb-lin_ All I do, I do, I do, Yes, all I

1. do, Lord, all I do. All I do, Lord, all I do.
2. do, Lord, all I do.

OH, MY GOOD LORD, SHOW ME DE WAY

To Mr. David Belasco

En - ter de char - i - ot, trav - el a - long.
En - ter de char - i - ot, trav - el a - long. Oh,

my good Lord, show me de way, Oh, my good Lord,

show me de way, Oh, my good Lord, show me de way,

En - ter de char - i - ot, trav - el a - long.

WERE YOU THERE WHEN THEY CRUCIFIED MY LORD?

To Mr. Will Marion Cook

Tenderly (*with deep emotion*)

Were you

there, when they cru - ci - fied my Lord?
there, when they nailed him to the tree?
there, when they pierced him in the side?
there, when the sun re - fused to shine?
there, when they laid him in the tomb?

Were you there, when they cru - ci - fied my
Were you there, when they nailed him to the
Were you there, when they pierced him in the
Were you there, when the sun - re - fused to
Were you there, when they laid him in the

137

CAN'T YOU LIVE HUMBLE!

To Mrs. Muriel Draper

MOS' DONE TOILIN' HERE

To Mr. Max Ewing

140

long to— shout, I love to sing— Mos' done toil-in' here. I

ain't been to heab'n, but I been tol'— Mos' done toil-in' here. De

love to— praise my heab'n-ly King, Mos' done toil-in' here. I

streets up— dere am paved wid gol',—Mos' done toil-in' here.

Hm—— Mos' done toil-in' here, O, bre-ther-en,

Hm—— Lord, I'm mos' done toil-in' here. here.

JUBALEE
(OR WHAT IS DE MATTER WID DE MOURNERS)

To my daughter Mildred

Jub - a - lee,   Jub - a - lee,   O, ____   my Lord! Jub - a - lee,

Jub - a - lee,   O,   Lord!   Jub - a - lee.   Jub - a - lee.

What is de mat-ter wid de mourn-ers, O,___ my Lord! De
What is de mat-ter wid ol' Zi-on, O,___ my Lord! You

dev-il's in de A-men cor-ner, O, Lord! Jub-a-lee.
bet-ter stop yo' fool-in' sin-ner man, O, Lord! Jub-a-lee.

Jub-a-lee, Jub-a-lee, O,___ my Lord! Jub-a-lee,

Jub-a-lee, O, Lord! Jub-a-lee. Jub-a-lee.

'ZEKIEL SAW DE WHEEL

To my wife, Nora E. Johnson

Wheel in de mid-dle of a wheel.
Wheel in de mid-dle of a wheel. 'Ze-kiel saw de wheel, 'Way up in de

mid-dle of de air, 'Ze-kiel saw de wheel. 'Way in de mid-dle of de

air. De big wheel run by faith, Lit-tle wheel run by de

grace of God; Wheel wid-in a wheel, 'Way in de mid-dle of de

145

146

WALK, MARY, DOWN DE LANE

To the memory of Ernest Hogan

Three long nights, an' three long days, Je-sus walk-in' down de lane.
In de morn - in' down de lane, In de morn-in' down de lane.

Three long nights, an' three long days, Je-sus walk-in' down de lane.
In de morn - in' down de lane, In de morn-in' down de lane.

Walk, Ma-ry, down de lane, — Walk, — Ma-ry, down de lane. —

Walk, Ma-ry, down de lane, — Walk, — Ma-ry, down de lane. — down de lane. —

Je-sus calls — you, down de lane, — Je-sus calls you, down de lane, —
In de heab'-n, down de lane, — In de heab'-n, down de lane, —
'fraid no-bod - y, down de lane, — 'Fraid no-bod-y, down de lane, —

Je-sus calls_you, down de lane,_ Je-sus_calls you, down de lane._
In de heab'-n, down de lane,_ In de_heab'-n, down de lane. I'm
'Fraid no-bod-y, down de lane,_ 'Fraid no-bod-y, _____ down de lane.

Walk, Ma-ry, down de lane,_ Walk,_Ma-ry, down de lane,_

Walk, Ma-ry, down de lane,_ Walk,_Ma-ry, down de lane._ down de lane._

MY SHIP IS ON DE OCEAN

To Mr. Stanley Spiegelberg

TO SEE GOD'S BLEEDIN' LAM'

To Mr. H. L. Mencken

Ja - cob's lad - der deep an' long, deep an' long, deep an' long;
See God's an - gel com - in' down, com - in' down, com - in' down;
Com - in' down in a sheet of blood, sheet of blood, sheet of blood;
Sheet of blood all min-gled wid fire, min-gled wid fire, min-gled wid fire;

Ja - cob's lad - der deep an' long,
See God's an - gel com - in' down,
Com - in' down in a sheet of blood, To see God's bleed-in' Lam'. Lam'.
Sheet of blood all min-gled wid fire,

Den you raise yo' voice up higher, voice up higher, voice up higher,
An' you jine dat heab'n-ly choir, heab'n-ly choir, heab'n-ly choir,

153

Den you raise yo' voice up higher,
An' you jine dat heab'n-ly choir, To see God's bleed-in' Lam'. Lam'. Yes, I

want to go to hea-b'n when I die,— when I die,— when I die; Yes, I

want to go to hea-b'n when I die, To see God's bleed-in' Lam'.____

MEMBERS, DON'T GIT WEARY

To the memory of Bert Williams

155

works mos' done. Mem-bers, done. O, keep yo'

lamp trim'd an' a - burn-in', Keep yo' lamp trim'd an' a - burn-in; Keep yo'

lamp trim'd an' a - burn-in' for de works mos' done. I'm gwine down

to de rib-buh ob Jor-dan, O, yes, gwine to de rib-buh ob
set at de wel-come ta-ble, O, yes, set at de wel-come
feas' on de milk an' hon-ey, O, yes, feas' on de milk an'
march wid de tall-es' an-gel, O, yes, march wid de tall-es'

Jor -dan, O, yes, gwine to de rib-buh ob Jor-dan, When my
ta -ble, O, yes, set at de wel - come ta - ble, When my
hon -ey, O, yes, feas' on de milk an' hon - ey, When my
an - gel, O, yes, march wid de tall - es' an - gel, When my

work is done. O, I'm gwine ___
work is done. O, I'm gwine ___ Mem - bers,
work is done. I'm gwine - ter ___
work is ___ done.

mf - pp

don't git wea - ry, Mem - bers, don't git wea - ry, Mem - bers,

don't git wea - ry for de work's mos' done. Mem - bers, done.

pp

I THANK GOD I'M FREE AT LAS'

To Mr. Heywood Broun

158

Way_ down yon-der in de grave yard walk, I thank God I'm free at las'_____
On - a my knees when de light pass by, I thank God I'm free at las'_____
Some o'dese morn - in's_ bright an' fair, I thank God I'm free at las' Gwine-ter

Me an' my Je-sus gwine ter meet an' talk,_ I thank God I'm free at las'
Tho't my soul would-a rise an' fly,_ I thank God I'm free at las'
meet my Je-sus in de mid-dle of de air,_ I thank God I'm _____

free at las! Free at las'_ free at las'_ I thank God I'm free at las'_

Free at las'_ free at las'_ I thank God I'm free at las! free at las'

DE OL' SHEEP DONE KNOW DE ROAD

(DE YOUNG LAM'S MUS' FIN' DE WAY)

To Mr. and Mrs. John E. Nail

fin' de way. Wid___ cros-ses an' trials__ on__ ev-'ry side, De
fin' de way. You'd__ bet-ter go git 'em 'fore you leave dis fiel,' De
fin' de way. For__ Christ__ has bought yo'__ lib-er-ty, De
fin' de way. Dat de Chris-tian has__ a__ right to shout, De

Repeat verses ad lib.

young lam's__ mus' fin' de way, My
young lam's__ mus' fin' de way, Oh,
young lam's__ mus' fin' de way, I
young lam's__ mus' fin' de way, Oh, de

ol' sheep done know de road, De ol' sheep done know de road, De ol' sheep done

know de road, De young lam's__ mus' fin' de way. Oh, de fin' de way.

DANIEL SAW DE STONE

To Mr. George Oppenheimer

Nev- ah saw such a man be- fo' Cut out de moun-tain wid-out hands.
Dan-iel pray'd in de li - on's den Cut out de moun-tain wid-out hands.
Pray'd an' pray'd three times a day Cut out de moun-tain wid-out hands. To

Preach-in' gos-pels to de po' Cut out de moun-tain wid-out hands.
Spite c' all dem wick-ed men, Cut out de moun-tain wid-out hands.
Drive de dev-il far a - way, Cut out de moun-tain wid-out hands.

Dan-iel saw de stone, Roll-in', roll-in', Dan-iel saw de

stone, Cut out de moun-tain wid-out hands.

I KNOW DE LORD'S LAID HIS HANDS ON ME

To Mr. Langston Hughes

O, I know de Lord, I know de Lord, I know de Lord's laid his hands on me; O, I know de Lord, I know de Lord, I know de Lord's laid his hands on me. O, hands on me. Did

ev - er you see de like be - fo' I know de Lord's laid his
was - n't a dat a hap - py day, I know de Lord's laid his
seek de Lord an' don't seek him right, I know de Lord's laid his
Lord has done jes' what He said, I know de Lord's laid his

164

hands on me; King Je - sus preach - in' to de po',____
hands on me; When Je - sus washed my sins a way,____
hands on me; Dey fool all day an' trifle all night,____
hands on me; He's healed de sick an' raised de dead,____

I know de Lord's laid his hands on me. O,
I know de Lord's laid his hands on me. Some
I know de Lord's laid his hands on me. My
I know de Lord's laid his hands on me. O,

I know de Lord,____ I know de Lord,____ I know de Lord's laid his hands on me. O,

I know de Lord,____ I know de Lord,____ I know de Lord's laid his hands on me. O hands on me.

165

OH, HEAR ME PRAYIN'
(LORD, FEED MY LAM'S)

To Mr. Winold Reiss

167

LOOK-A HOW DEY DONE MY LORD

To Mr. Guy Johnson

170

DERE'S A HAN'WRITIN' ON DE WALL

To Mr. and Mrs. Percy Hammond

want - in' Dere's a han' writ - in' on de wall, _____ Dere's a

han' writ - in' on de wall, _____ Dere's a han'

writ - in' on de wall. _____ Oh, won't you come an' read it,

See what _ it say, Dere's a han' writ - in' on de wall. _____

I FEEL LIKE MY TIME AIN'T LONG

To Mrs. Irita Van Doren

Moderato (*with pathos*)

I feel like, — I feel like, Lord, — I feel like my time ain't long; — I feel like, — I feel like, Lord, — I feel like my time ain't long. — I long. —

1. Went to de grave-yard de
2. Some-times I'm up — an' some-
3. Mind out, my broth-er, how you

174

oth-er day,— I feel like my time ain't long,— I looked at de place where my
times I'm down,— I feel like my time ain't long,— An' some-times I'm al-mos'—
walk de cross,— I feel like my time ain't long,— Yo' foot might slip — an' yo'

moth-er lay, — I feel like my time ain't long. —
on-de groun' — I feel like my time ain't long. — I
soul git los' — I feel like my time ain't long. —

feel like, — I feel like, Lord, I feel like my time ain't long; — I

feel like, — I feel like, Lord, I feel like my time ain't long. — I long. —

175

COME HERE LORD!

To Mr. Harry Block

Moderately Fast

Come here,— Lord!—

Come here,—— Lord! —— Come here,—— Lord! —— Sin - ner cry - in'

come here, Lord. come here, Lord. O

lit - tle did I think He was so nigh,
mourn —— ers —— if you will be - lieve,
seek —— God's face but don't seek right,
sin - ner you had bet - ter pray,

Sin-ner cry-in' come here, Lord. He spoke- an' He made me laugh an' cry,
Sin-ner cry-in' come here, Lord. De grace- of — God you will re-ceive,
Sin-ner cry-in' come here, Lord. Dey pray a lit'le by day an' none by night,
Sin-ner cry-in' come here, Lord. For Sa- tan's 'round you ev -'ry day,

Sin - ner cry - in' come here, Lord. O,
Sin - ner cry - in' come here, Lord. Some come here, Lord. Come here, —
Sin - ner cry - in' come here, Lord. O,
Sin - ner cry - in'

Lord! — Come here, — Lord! — Come here, —

Lord! — Sin - ner cry - in' come here, Lord. come here, Lord.

HOL' DE WIN' DON'T LET IT BLOW

To Mr. and Mrs. Eugene Goossens

Moderately Lively

Hol' de win':

Hol' de win'! Hol' de win' don't let it blow;— Hol' de win'!

Hol' de win'!— Hol' de win' don't let it blow. let it blow.

Talk a-bout me jes' as much as you please, Hol' de win' don't
You ask me why I kin shout-a so boï, Hol' de win' don't
You ask me why I am al-ways so glad, Hol' de win' don't
I'm gwine to hea-b'n an' I'm gwine dere right, Hol' de win' don't

178

let it blow; — De more you talk I'm gwine-ter ben' my knees,
let it blow; — De love of Je - sus sho' is in my soul,
let it blow; — De dev - il missed de soul he tho't he had,
let it blow; — I'm gwine to hea - b'n all - a dressed in white,

Hol' de win' don't let it blow.
Hol' de win' don't let it blow. let it blow. Hol' de win'!
Hol' de win' don't let it blow.
Hol' de win' don't

Hol' de win'! Hol' de win' don't let it blow; — Hol' de win'!

Hol' de win'! — Hol' de win' don't let it blow. let it blow.

WALK TOGETHER CHILDREN

To Dr. W. E. Burghardt DuBois

mourn   and nev - er   tire; _____

Mourn   and   nev - er   tire. _____

Mourn   and   nev - er   tire; _____   There's a

great camp - meet - ing in the Prom - ised Land. Gwine - ter   Land. Oh,

HUMBLE YO'SELF DE BELL DONE RING

To my Coadjutor—Taylor Gordon

Praise de Lord! Glo-ry and hon-or! Praise King Je-sus! Glo-ry an' hon-or!

Praise de Lord! Oh, my young Christians I got lots for to tell you,

Je-sus Christ speak-in' thro' de or-gans of de clay. ("One day, one

day, Lord!") God's gwine-ter call dem chil-lun fom a dis-tant lan!

Tomb-stones a-crack-in' graves a-bust-in' Hell an' de sea am gwine-ter give up de dead.

False pre-ten-der wears sheep cloth-in' on his back, In his heart he's like a

rav - in' wolf.__ ("Judge ye not, brother,") For ye shall be

judged false pre-ten-der git-tin' in de Chris-tian band. Glo-ry an' hon-or!

186

See God 'n' you see God 'n' you see God in de morn-in', He'll come a-rid-in' on de line of time.— De fire'll be fall-in', He'll be call-in' "Come to judg-a-ment come". Live-a hum-ble,— hum-ble,— Lord! Hum-ble yo'self, de bell done ring; Live-a hum-ble,— hum-ble,— Lord!

CPSIA information can be obtained
at www.ICGtesting.com
Printed in the USA
LVHW100744271019
635357LV00025B/119/P

9 780306 812026